Sex and the Outer Planets

Barbara H. Watters

Copyright 2010 by American Federation of Astrologers, Inc.

No part of this book may be reproduced or transcribed in any form or by any means, electronic or mechanical, including photocopying or recording or by any information storage and retrieval system without written permission from the author and publisher, except in the case of brief quotations embodied in critical reviews and articles. Requests and inquiries may be mailed to: American Federation of Astrologers, Inc., 6535 S. Rural Road, Tempe, AZ 85283.

ISBN-10: 0-86690-604-5
ISBN-13: 978-0-86690-604-3

Cover Design: Jack Cipolla

www.astrologers.com

Published by:
American Federation of Astrologers, Inc.
6535 S. Rural Road
Tempe, AZ 85283

Printed in the United States of America

Contents

Chapter I, The Inner Planets	1
Chapter II, The Middle Planets	7
Chapter III, The Expanding Universe	17
Chapter IV, Sexual Distortion in the Saturn-Dominated Chart	23
Adolf Hitler	23
The Marquis de Sade	32
Chapter V, Sexual Distortion in the Jupiter-Dominated Chart	35
Chapter VI, The Outer Planets	45
Uranus	45
Neptune	52
Pluto	56
Chapter VII, Uranus as a Sex Significator	65
Homosexuality—Rebellion	65
Somerset Maugham and Gertrude Stein	73
Chapter VIII, Neptune As a Sex Significator	77
Masochism	77
Impotence	88
Chapter IX, Pluto as a Sex Significator	93
Violence and Delinquency	93
Rape	102

Chapter X, Pluto and Genius	107
Sublimation of Sex and Violence	107
Louis Pasteur	110
Vincent Van Gogh	112
Eugene O'Neill	115
Appendix A, Formula for Casting Johndro Birth Locality Charts	119
Appendix B, Data Sources	121

Illustrations

Foundation Chart of European Civilization	18
Chart of Adolf Hitler	24
Johndro Chart of the Marquis de Sade	33
Chart of Sigmund Freud	36
Foundation Chart of the United States	47
Johndro Chart of Somerset Maugham	74
Johndro Chart of Gertrude Stein	75
Johndro Chart of Jean-Jacques Rousseau	84
Solar Chart of Clyde Barrow	100
Solar Chart of Bonnie Parker	101
Johndro Chart of Albert DeSalvo	103
Chart of Louis Pasteur	111
Chart of Vincent Van Gogh	113
Chart of Eugene O'Neill	115

Chapter I

The Inner Planets

Astrologers divide the heavenly bodies of the solar system into three groups. This division was arrived at empirically, by observation of the apparent effect of the different bodies on human beings and human affairs.

The first group is the largest. It includes the Sun and the Moon, which in astrology are known as the Lights. The planets included are Mercury, Venus, and Mars. These five bodies are called the *personal* planets. Their placement in the signs of the zodiac and in the houses of horoscope describe innate temperament, feeling about self and others, and personal reactions to the everyday circumstances of life. These are the planets of freewill, the ones that offer personal choices that are in our control.

Since these inner planets are mainly concerned with our feelings and reactions to the normal, taken-for-granted circumstances of our daily lives, they present us with the opportunity to say yes, no, or maybe. If we do not use these opportunities to make decisions freely about our personal lives and reactions to others, it may be because we have allowed ourselves to become trapped in habits. If so, we can change those habits and learn new ones that suit us better. Or it may be that one of the middle or outer planets is exerting pressure upon us from circumstances we did not make and cannot control.

For instance, the planet Mercury rules all forms of verbal written and printed communication. Most people living today in the United States are deluged with a constant stream of mercurial verbiage. This verbiage comes to us from outside our limited sphere of personal activity; it is generated in the larger field we call society and is a product of the strong emphasis on Mercury and the sign Gemini in the horoscope of the United States. We are not free to change that. Nevertheless, because this endless stream of words is Mercury-ruled, we are free to decide how we will react to it. We cannot stop the junk mail from coming, but we do not have to read it. We cannot stop the radio announcer from talking, but we do not have to listen to him. As individuals, we cannot change the content of a single book, magazine, or newspaper; but we do not have to buy any of them which do not please us.

It is easy to imagine a mercurial situation that is exactly the reverse. We might have been born into an illiterate society where all printed matter was unknown, or into some prehistoric time before writing was invented. Once more, the larger field of reality—the primitive society—would limit the freedom of our wills. While no amount of wishing would bring a stream of junk mail to the door of early Egyptians, they were free to choose or reject other mercurial values. They could develop great manual dexterity in various handcrafts, spend evenings listening to story-tellers, or teach the traditions of their culture to the young so that traditions would be passed on from generation to generation.

These mercurial choices of the prehistoric Egyptian are not as readily available to us. Our society presses against us from all sides to buy mass-produced items rather than "waste time" making them; to look at television rather than read a book; or to learn how to earn a living, rather than waste time with ancient history, which has limited use. Many people regard storytelling and the cultivation of cultural traditions in the young as impractical.

The question of which type of society produces the wiser or happier human being is a moot point, because where we have the maximum freedom of choice about every day activities, a larger field of reality that we do not control dictates to us in countless ways that limit our choices. This social dictation comes from planets that lie beyond the orbit of Mars. We are usually unaware of the limitations society and custom set upon the freedom of our wills. We are trained in infancy to adapt to the limitations our society imposes, and we grow up accepting them. At times, we even go to war (Mars) to defend them. Yet, within the limits of our social constraint, we all make countless free decisions every day. Some of these decisions, although they seem unimportant at the time, may have far-reaching results in our lives.

The most important consequences of our use of inner planet freewill are a result of how we behave toward other people.

Other people tend to like those of us born with the Moon trine to Venus, because we treat them courteously, with tact and consideration. We can also become so busy with parties and other people's affairs that there is little time to work unless freewill is used to say no to some of the fun and games.

Many people find those of us born with the Moon square the Sun to be "difficult," and treat us in ways that can create trouble. This is because Moon square Sun people often feel cantankerous and impulsively tell people off in no uncertain fashion. It is quite possible, however, to curb impulse and practice tact and consideration. Obviously, no matter what kind of society we live in, such an exertion of freewill can have important consequences; it might even cause career changes.

Among the inner planets, Mars and Venus are the *heterosexual* significators. Mars describes the sex impulses of the normal male, and Venus those of the normal female. This is true for all human beings, regardless of the society, class, race, or era in which they are born. It is rash to say that where biology is concerned we have much freewill. In late adolescence, normal people will feel a strong urge to couple with a member of the opposite sex, and they have little control over feeling the urge. In our society, we are encouraged to believe that we may choose our mates freely. This means that our social codes of morality approve of marriages for love, but frown on marriages for money, status, or those forced by parental pressure. Americans are brought up to believe that marriage is a purely personal affair. Few other societies in the history of humanity have maintained this point of view and taught it to the young. In most other times and places, marriage was regarded as a social contract and a family affair. Marriages were arranged for reasons that had nothing to do with love, and neither party to the bargain had any choice in the matter.

However benighted and strange they may seem to us, social customs are seldom wholly unreasonable. The negotiated marriage was usually arranged to occur in late adolescence, when the Mars-Venus biological urge was at its height. The negotiated marriage gave social sanction to sexual fulfillment at the very time the need for it was most insistent. Society assumed the young couple would enjoy each other and produce many children. Beyond that, they were free to learn to love each other or not, as they chose. Society was not concerned with love, but solely with the Mars-Venus sex principle and its normal fulfillment.

The Sun and Moon are the significators of love, Mars and Venus of the *love affair*. Through the Sun and Moon we love many people who are not objects of sexual desire: friends, parents, children, even some relatives. It is also through the Sun and Moon that the Mars-Venus sex relation deepens into love.

In the United States, the pressure brought against the young to marry someone of their own choice for love means that most of them marry under the strong compulsion of the Mars-Venus sex impulse, thinking that it is love. This may be the principal reason for our high divorce rate. People who believe that the desire to make love to someone is the same as loving that person will often find themselves emotionally starved. The Sun-Moon capacity to love and cherish another unselfishly will not be fulfilled. Its lack of fulfillment creates a great hunger in the spirit that only love can satisfy. Such people, thinking the Mars-Venus desire to make love is love itself, move on from mate to mate, until they become emotional skeletons, incapable of loving anyone.

The astrologer is asked to help solve more problems concerning love, marriage, and sex than any others.

Therefore, before trying to help friends, clients, or ourselves through astrology, it is well to remember that a Venus-Mars conjunction between two charts creates the desire for physical satisfaction. A Sun-Moon conjunction between two charts creates the possibility of emotional fulfillment, on some level, even if physical desire is absent.

The Mars-Venus attachment is a biologically conditioned impulse that we are free to give in to it or not, as we choose. Between the ages of eighteen and twenty-five, the Mars-Venus impulse is diffuse. It is a normal need of the organism during these years, which can become so strong that any person of the opposite sex who is available becomes an object of desire. This is called "falling in love." It is not uncommon for a young person to fall in love a dozen times in a few years if the biological need for a mate remains unsatisfied. During these years of our lives we are not free *not* to feel this impulse, and the chart of young person who does not feel should be studied with sympathy and great consideration. However, the impulse to find sexual satisfaction should not be confused with love.

People cannot learn to feel the Mars-Venus desire for heterosexual satisfaction. Many sexual hangups and aberrations occur because of contacts from the outer planets with Mars or Venus in a chart. Freewill occurs in the recognition that normal biological impulses can be warped and distorted. This is most apt to come about through frustration of the Sun-Moon impulse to find emotional fulfillment in love. It is probably possible for all human beings to learn to love at least one other person, provided the difference between love and sex is understand. But to teach oneself to love another, the longing for emotional fulfillment must be strong. The will is free to learn the lesson, but sometimes it is so difficult to learn that we settle for persuading ourselves we do not want something that is so hard to get.

As students of astrology, we should also recognize that there are times when configurations between the outer planets are so powerful and stressful that no society can withstand the radical changes they bring. Then a generation of children will be born with that same great stress in their own horoscopes. They will grow up in societies that are torn by war, anarchy, decadence, corruption, revolution, and technological changes too rapid to assimilate. Society will have no authority over them because, under the onslaught of stressful events, it cannot regulate or discipline itself. Children born into such anarchy have the greatest difficulty in learning to love anyone. A society in the throes of revolutionary anarchy and rapid change becomes unreliable, dangerous—like a jungle. It ceases to fulfill the first obligation of society, which is to protect and nourish the people who form it.

Where society has no stability, anything goes. Everyone feels that most of what we know today will be gone tomorrow. In such an environment, it is hard to learn to love and easy to learn to hate. Love is a lifetime commitment. Hate, like the Mars-Venus sex urge, is diffuse and can change its object at will.

The angles of relationship (aspects) formed between the outer planets persist for several years. Therefore, many people are born with the same stresses that the angles represent. If these stresses also afflict the Sun or Moon of a horoscope, the individual will feel strong emotional pressures from society. Early in life, these individuals may become alienated from their environments, families, and all the people and institutions that should have authority over them.

The Sun symbolizes authority we must respect. Where it is badly afflicted, all authority seems tyrannical and unworthy of respect: it inspires only fear. The reaction to persistent fear of something we cannot change is suppressed rage and self-hatred. This stress may become so unbearable that the desire for relief from inner tension takes the form of irrational violence. We can become professional haters, shut off from the desire to learn to love. When this happens, personal will (the Sun) becomes atrophied and warped and all subsequent behavior and motivations are affected.

Since about 1930, the outer planets have repeatedly formed long-lasting, stressful aspects to each other. Millions of people have been born with these aspects. Therefore, they cannot be considered personal unless they also afflict the personal, inner planets in the individual horoscope. Groups of people born since 1930, and especially those born during the 1940s, comprise the alienated generations. Individuals are alienated to the degree that stressful patterns formed between the outer planets afflict the personal, inner planets of their charts. When such afflictions are great and numerous, these individuals may feel no freedom to make choices about anything, or even feel very much like a person. Relief from emotional starvation is sought through running with gangs, huddling in communes, joining movements, and stilling fears with drugs. Those who feel no will of their own seek direction from something outside, something big, amorphous, and all powerful and find it in the dominant outer planets.

6/Sex and the Outer Planets

Chapter II

The Middle Planets

The middle planets are Jupiter and Saturn. With the exception of the Sun, these are the two largest bodies in the solar system. Because of their enormous size, the regularity of their orbits, and the vast extent of their gravitational fields, they act like two great balance wheels to stabilize the system and keep celestial order in it. In the symbolism of astrology, they are considered to serve the same function in human affairs.

The orbits of Jupiter and Saturn around the Sun are slow enough for us to experience their influence as an orderly change, yet fast enough for us to perceive that things do change. Jupiter's orbit is twelve earth years. He remains almost exactly one year in each sign of the zodiac (slightly less in Libra and Scorpio, slightly more in Aries and Taurus). Saturn's orbit through the signs is a little less than thirty earth years, and he remains almost two and one-half years in each sign. If we assume a life span is seventy years, a human being will experience five revolutions of Jupiter and two of Saturn. This means that as Jupiter moves through the heavens, it will make every possible aspect to every planet in a natal chart five times. Saturn will do the same twice.

Because of this orderly repetition, bringing a recurrence of similar experiences into our lives at stated intervals, Jupiter and Saturn are considered to be the preceptors of the zodiac. They not only give us the opportunity to learn through experience, they also give us the chance to use what we learned the next time around.

Together they symbolize the process of maturation on all levels of human existence: biological, mental, spiritual, and social. This process of maturation that Jupiter and Saturn control is orderly and normal. It predictably occurs to a greater or lesser degree in the development of every human being as a concomitant of the process of living, and each stage of the process occurs, ideally, at the same time in every life. For this reason, Jupiter and Saturn are considered to be the regulators of cosmic law as it affects human beings.

These two patriarchs of the zodiac symbolize exactly opposite principles. Operating together, they achieve a system of checks and balances, the goal of which is a golden mean of correct proportion, a middle ground of normality. Jupiter symbolizes the principle of growth and expansion, while Saturn represents the principle of limitation and boundaries. Jupiter creates the codes of law, ethics, and culture by which we live; Saturn enforces discipline when we break the codes and punishes us when we infringe them. Saturn creates the ties of necessity that bind us to each other, to our responsibilities, and to the limitations of our human condition; Jupiter loosens the bonds when they become so tight that they endanger our further growth. Jupiter symbolizes plenty; Saturn, want. Jupiter is our flesh, Saturn our bones. Jupiter is what we build; Saturn is the foundation on which we build it. Jupiter is leisure; Saturn is work. Jupiter sends us traveling; Saturn brings us home. Jupiter is the eternal optimist; Saturn, the pessimist. Jupiter gambles, Saturn hoards. Jupiter gives, Saturn takes. Jupiter is the sower, Saturn the reaper. Jupiter extends credit, Saturn collects the bill. Jupiter is spirit, Saturn is matter. Jupiter is eternity. Saturn is time that is parceled out. Each of us gets an allotted span of minutes—so much, and no more. Jupiter is reincarnation. Saturn is karma.

Neither planet, if operating in its proper sphere, is a sex significator. But either planet may take on secondary sexual significance and symbolism if its primary functions are distorted or inhibited. Such distortion or inhibition may arise if either planet forms strong stressful aspects to the personal inner planets while it also receives stressful aspects from one or more of the outer planets. When Jupiter is under stress, facts become distorted and over-optimism may lead to reckless behavior, such as a tendency to gamble or indiscriminant involvement in casual affairs that prove detrimental to the health or finances. Jupiter is emotionally shallow. When it is the strongest planet in the chart, both the personality and character may suffer from the inability to form deep, lasting attachments.

Since the basic nature of the planet is emotional shallowness, individuals who have these stressful aspects are not likely to realize what is missing. Their happy-go-lucky, here-today-gone-tomorrow natures convince everyone, including themselves, that they are happy people.

Saturn is emotionally cold, and at the same time greedy. When Saturn afflicts the inner planets—especially the Moon, Venus, or Mars—it inhibits the freedom of choice in emotional matters. If, at the same time, it also receives stress from one or more of the outer planets, the inhibition may be so severe as to result in distortions of values and displacement of the emotions upon material things or worldly power. A dominant Saturn, influencing both inner and outer planets, indicates a psychological complex or physical condition that inhibits normal sexual expression, and may even forbid the will to desire it. Any people who were permanently crippled in childhood by accident, disease, or some congenital defect have horoscopes with this type of Saturn. They may be capable of great and lasting love, but, be unable to express their affection through sex because of their physical condition.

More commonly, Saturnian afflictions show emotional warping through the influence of a dominating parent, a cruel and exacting one, or the loss of a parent at an early age. Through no fault of the child, the lack of something vital causes emotional warping that interferes with proper development. If a child happens to be born with a brutal father, an over-possessive mother, or defective genes, the child can do nothing to change the situation or repair the damage. While freedom of will might still operate to persuade a child to choose a constructive, rather than a destructive, adaptation, the freedom to choose a course of action in infancy that would replace a dead parent with a living one, a bad parent with a good one, or extreme poverty with plenty does not exist.

Saturnian afflictions to personal planets operate to deprive us of something necessary to the normal process of maturation. The privation may be physical, mental, emotional, economic, or social. But it always comes from some condition outside ourselves and operates as an external fact we are powerless to change. The effects are not subjective. The external world in which the causes are rooted is not subjective. The distortions of development caused by severe Saturnian privations or frustrations leave permanent scars. Saturn is the lord of the irreparable damage, the chronic and incurable. We are forced to accept and live with whatever Saturn brings us through his contacts with our inner planets. We cannot change it by any exercise of freewill, any more than we can stop our bodies from maturing, growing old, and dying. We can accept the process, resent it, try to hasten or delay it; but we are not free to change it.

Jupiter afflictions come in pleasant disguises. Saturn afflictions do not. Those who suffer from them are consciously aware of some profound lack in their lives or in their development. Therefore, we react to Saturn afflictions, as we do not to those from Jupiter. The remnants of freewill Saturn leaves in the inner planets he afflicts, we use to decide what our attitudes toward our afflictions will be.

First, we can recognize and accept difficult conditions and try to live as fully and freely as possible within the limits imposed. This results in counting our blessings even though others may think we have none to count.

Second, we can refuse to mentally accept difficult conditions, although we know they are real. We then become liars and neurotics who defend ourselves from reality by trying to replace it with a subjective world that exists only in our own minds. Things seldom go right for people who deny reality because, as time passes, they become severely warped emotionally. Their judgments of their real situations in the world become distorted.

Third, after accepting the condition, we can try to compensate for it by developing talents left unimpaired, or even enhanced by the condition. Many people who choose this course become great, like Helen Keller or Franklin Roosevelt.

Fourth, we can deny the true nature of the privation and substitute for it something else that we are able to get in abundance. This is a common choice. It results in overcompensation with an excessive appetite for something symbolic of the original lack. But this substitute can never fill the lack, however much of it we get, because it is always something quite different in its very nature from the thing we were originally deprived of. Usually, people who choose this course suffered emotional privation in childhood. Many become compulsive eaters, drinkers, drug addicts, power seekers, money makers, or tyrants.

If some of the outer planets join in the afflictions, the overcompensation may be excessive violence, or some sexual aberration associated with brutality. Hitler, Goebbels, Robespierre, and Napoleon were all people of this type who made this choice. But no amount of power or bloodletting could compensate Hitler or Robespierre for their emotional deadness, Goebbels for his club foot, or Napoleon for his small stature.

When a strong Saturn warps or frustrates the normal sexual development, it becomes a sex significator in the chart. If overcompensation is sought through sex, the person may become coldly, lustful, and insatiable. Or, indifferent to sex, the person may use it to make money, as do pimps, whores, and brothel-keepers. The murderer Landru seduced and killed many women for their money.

Saturn as a sex significator may describe a wide range of abnormalities, distortions, and compensations, depending upon the whole chart. This is bound to be so because, as a sex significator, Saturn is playing a role unsuited to his true nature. Therefore, he can assume almost any disguise—none of them fortunate. There may be total inhibition: impotence, extreme Puritanism, or frigidity. There may be sex or marriage for gain of status. There may be cruelty, excessive lust, violence, child molesting, or incest. Any indication that Saturn is being used as a sex significator calls for the most careful examination of the whole chart.

During the development of primitive and classical astrology and astronomy—a period of about five thousand years—Saturn marked the outer limits of the universe in the knowledge and psychology of human beings. The symbolism used in astrology to describe the nature and activity of Saturn was inevitably influenced by this fact. As the Lord of the Universal Boundaries, he was the final arbiter in all mundane affairs. There was no appeal from his judgments. There could not be because only the abyss lay beyond him. He was therefore the symbol of the inexorable power of the Karmic Law, which demanded an exact accounting, in the fullness of time, for every action. He was called the Reaper, because he forced men to harvest exactly the crop they sowed. Any man or nation that tried arrogantly to push beyond the limits of Saturn was guilty of the overweening pride the Greeks called *hybris*. Always, as they reached the peak of power, Saturn hurled them into the abyss. It did not matter whether their names were Alexander, Hitler, or the Roman Empire. Saturn was no respecter of names when he recognized an absence of humility.

Both Saturn and Jupiter impressed the ancient and classical astrologers as agents of fatality. In stressful aspects to the inner planets, these planets brought troubles that were often greater than deserved or perhaps not deserved at all. When they formed fortunate aspects, they often seemed to reward the wicked far beyond their merits. It also became obvious very early that the rewards and punishments were connected with social, political, and economic factors beyond the individual's control. A lucky, elevated Jupiter seemed to grant success through accidental circumstances, like high birth, powerful friends, or lucky breaks that brought favorable public notice. An elevated, fortunate Saturn had much the same effect, except that it raised up people who were often of lowly origin and had to work hard to get and keep the opportunities that promoted them. It was clear that people had some freedom of choice in adjusting to the effects of Jupiter and Saturn, but limited freedom to adjust to situations beyond our control is hardly the same thing as freedom of the will to *create* situations that please or encourage us.

For these and many other reasons based in observation and analogy, Jupiter and Saturn were assigned to the control of the social, political, and economic spheres. Just as they governed the *normal* process of maturation of the human body, mind, and career, they controlled the *normal* processes of social development and the *regular* political and economic cycles, which, because of their very regularity, assured that when change occurred it would be orderly and would not disrupt the society, or throw it into anarchy. Just as Jupiter and Saturn were the great balance wheels of the solar system, so were they the great balance wheels of society. Operating together according to a predictable system of cosmic law, these two planets provided the checks and balances that assured the development of both individuals and societies toward a normal mean in relation to their environments.

Bad harvest years were succeeded by good ones, and vice versa. Inflation was followed by deflation. The excessive expansion of power was followed by disastrous defeats in war and the fragmentation of empires. Anarchy was followed by tyranny. The king died and his heir was crowned. The ages-old shout of the populace roared through the streets: "The king is dead! Long live the king!" It was acknowledgment that although people passed away, the State endured. It was also a prayer that nothing in the mysterious outer darkness of the abyss would disturb the two great gods in their appointed rounds, which might cause them to become irresponsible and derelict of their duty to keep law and order in the universe.

As above, so below.

During the thousands of years when people believed that Jupiter and Saturn were the outer planets, the final arbiters of authority, law, and fate, the human imagination was limited in its concepts of human and social possibilities. The ideal society was one in which law, order, and custom were automatically regulated by a hierarchy of status. The ideal human life was one in which the individual had a secure place in this hierarchy, knew exactly what it was, and lived according to customs proper for that station. A person's place in the hierarchy—whether king, nobleman, artisan, serf, slave, female chattel, rich, or poor—was largely determined by accidents of birth. People are born in certain families, tribes, or nations, and are either "well-born" or bastards. A man married to increase his holdings or to enhance his wealth or status. Women were sold to the highest bidder for the same reasons. Within the lawful bonds of matrimony or legal concubinage, the only *proper* function of sex was to produce children, who were valuable commodities. Children assured the continuity of bloodlines, they could be bargained off in marriage to increase the family's wealth or power, and they provided more hands to work on the land or in the family business.

In all such status regulated societies, regardless of their historical era or geographical location, there were two occupations that were somewhat outside the rigid, automatic control of the status order. These were the priesthood and trade. A man, and sometimes a woman, could choose to enter one of these occupations through an exercise of freewill, even though he or she had been born into a recognized social class. Once in the priesthood or trade, the person could rise in its internal hierarchy through personal efforts and become rich or powerful in spite of origins that may have been lowly.

In all status societies, the priesthood formed a ruling caste whose power existed outside earthly law and was exercised parallel to and outside the power of kings and governments. In most places and periods, kings themselves had to submit to the priesthood or risk losing their kingdoms through the magic powers the priests could exert against them. Also in most times and places, the codes of sexual morality were dictated by and enforced by the established religion the priesthood administered. The enforcement of the sexual code of morality was one of the most important functions of the priesthood in every patriarchal society. The reason is obvious: all such societies depend for their stability upon the orderly transference of property and power from the father to the *rightful* heir. Wherever status and power descend from father to son, the chastity of the mother becomes a primary concern of society. Maternity is a matter of fact; paternity is an article of faith.

In all these societies, where the limits of possible development are set by Saturn as the outer boundary, the chastity of the female becomes the cornerstone of the socially accepted code of sexual morality. To enforce female chastity, the legal status of women is the same as that of slaves or serfs. As chattels, they have no choice about what will be done with their bodies, or who will become their sexual masters. Abortion and birth control are both crimes in the same category as murder. All sexual expression except for the propagation of children is sinful in the female. Rape is a crime of which the woman alone is guilty. Women are legally forbidden to own property except as a dower right (when the husband administers it), or in the rare times and places when they may rule kingdoms. By social consent, and sometimes by law, they are deprived of any means of earning a living except in some domestic capacity or menial trade. Their only excuse for existence, and the sole reason for their preservation in the society, is their indispensable function as child bearers. Both a woman's life and her honor depend upon her recognition of this and her acceptance of it.

If she infringes the code, she is either killed or becomes an outcast, which means a thief or a prostitute or both. Sex as an adventure or a pleasurable activity is the prerogative of males only, who are entitled to all they can get of it outside the bonds of matrimony; and, in polygamous societies, within them. While the male satisfies most of his sexual needs with prostitutes, all women, regardless of their station, are fair game to hunt down and capture if he can. It is up to the women to protect their bodies from unlicensed intruders. If they fail to do so, they are ostracized from society or killed. The only respectable alternative to marriage provided by some of these societies is a career as a religious. Both Christianity and Buddhism tolerate nuns. Many pagan religions tolerated priestesses. But Islam, Judaism, and Hinduism have no place for women in their religious orders, although some Hindu sects accepted them as temple prostitutes.

The effect of the Jupiter-Saturn sexual codes of morality upon the society was tremendous. Over the centuries and millennia, the code became so deeply embedded in the laws, institutions, and social customs of most societies that neither the imagination nor psychology of the people could conceive of social structures where it did not operate. It was right, normal, and natural; anything else was wrong, abnormal, unnatural, and contrary to divine law. The psychology and emotions of every human being were so profoundly conditioned by the Saturn-Jupiter moral code that if so much as a thought or a dream infringed it, the person felt guilty. Since many of the thoughts, dreams and impulses about sex were quite natural and inevitable because they were rooted in the condition of being human—that is, in the personal planets—children grew up imagining that they were guilty vessels of all sorts of unimaginable sins. The historical and cultural affects that the creation of countless guilt-ridden people had upon the Jupiter-Saturn society has been profound.

Of course, it never crossed anyone's mind that the moral code might be unduly restrictive. To imagine even the possibility of a different code goes beyond the boundaries of Saturn, which was impossible. Therefore, people living under the Jupiter-Saturn code cannot be blamed for failing to realize that neither is a sex planet. To create codes and enforce laws are proper functions of these planets. But to call upon them to create codes and enforce laws that regulate every thought, whim, and expression of human sexual activity is to demand too much of them, for no authority can regulate values it does not understand. When Saturn and Jupiter were forced to do this for thousands of years, they became guilty of the very *hybris* it was part of their function to punish.

Sex and love are meaningless values for Jupiter and Saturn. When forced to administer them, the result was, and still is, disaster. Their reign over sexual morality resulted in hideous aberrations of sexual expression in the whole society, exactly as it does in the individual when these planets assume sexual dominance over the horoscope. One of the commonest aberrations that results from distortion of sex values into patterns of suppressed guilt is cruelty. As they age, all the Jupiter-Saturn controlled societies become abnormally cruel. With the sanction of the established religion, they develop sadistic legal codes, systems of legal torture that function with cold, Saturnian efficiency. They legalize inhuman treatment of women, children, heretics, outcasts, prisoners, and anyone else who is powerless to resist.

The most notable example of this social phenomenon in recent history is the Jupiter-Saturn reign of the Inquisition, which lasted for about six centuries. It warped and distorted the whole development of Europe, exactly as a Saturnian affliction in infancy may warp the development of children's bones, condemning them to be "cripples" for life. Hitler, whose personal planets were afflicted by Saturn, attempted a regression to this sort of society. The planets beyond Saturn, and countries dominated by them, assured his downfall.

Saturn and Jupiter will always fail when given rulership over sexual morality, whether by societies or by individuals, because, mighty as they are, they are not mightier than the Sun, which rules the principle of love. Nor do they have much influence upon the motion of Earth's satellite, the Moon, which rules the principle of sympathy (the impulse of one human being to care what happens to another). And although they may grievously distort the natural expression of Mars and Venus, in the final analysis, it is beyond their powers ever to kill the deep, primordial urge of the human being to assure the continuance of the human race.

The evidence that shows the limits of their powers is this: every so often in mankind's checkered history, one of their efficient, well-regulated, rationally ordered societies breaks down and is thrown into anarchy. The first thing that happens in any society with the onset of anarchy is a wild upsurge of sexuality and sexual license. The Jupiter-Saturn sexual code of morality is torn into shreds and thrown in the trash bin. Homosexuals come out of hiding. Nuns and priests abjure their vows. The young marry for love. Women struggle against the bonds of chattel slavery. And sex becomes respectable.

Saturn was the patron god of Rome. His rule was rigid, his discipline strict. Every year, when the Sun entered the sign of Capricorn, the Romans celebrated a festival in his honor, called the Saturnalia. During the days of the festival, slaves were treated as free people, thus tasting liberty from the bondage of Saturn. Everyone gave gifts to their friends and family and forgave their debtors, thus temporarily counteracting Saturn's stingy greed. And at the height of the festival, everyone who wished to participated in sex orgies, thus briefly defying Saturnian repression. These mild antidotes were not enough, perhaps, but they were more than most other Jupiter-Saturn societies have had. This may help to explain why the Roman State lasted longer than most Jupiter-Saturn societies.

16/Sex and the Outer Planets

Chapter III

The Expanding Universe

The European civilization suffered the full brunt of traumatic effect from the discovery of the planets beyond Saturn. The classical Graeco-Roman civilization that preceded it had lasted from about 800 BC, when Greece began to emerge from its Dark Age of barbarism, to about AD 400, when the Gothic hordes over-ran the Roman Empire. Four hundred years of anarchy and barbarian war followed.

Finally, Charles the Great, one of the most ruthless conquerors Europe ever produced, subdued all the other warlords and converted them, by force, to Christianity. By 804 BC, he controlled all Europe from the Pyrenees to the Elbe and the Danube; and from the English Channel to the Mediterranean. The British Isles, Spain, the southern tip of Italy, Sicily, and Sardinia lay outside his dominions, as did the Scandinavian countries. Therefore, the foundation chart for European civilization does not apply to them. England, Scotland, Wales, and Scandinavia remained pagan. Spain, Sardinia, and Sicily were under the control of Islam.

On Christmas Day, in the year 800 BC, Charles the Great was crowned Holy Roman Emperor by Pope Leo III. The chart for this event was constructed by Ralph Kraum. It is of great interest to astrologers because it is one of only two authentic horoscopes for the birth of a civilization. The other is the chart for the beginning of the Mohammedan Era.

The State that Charlemagne created under the auspices of this chart had all the outward form and institutional structure of the Jupiter-Saturn society. The form was hierarchical feudalism. The warlords who owned land were semi-autonomous nobles who owed allegiance to the emperor. Below them in the class structure were the warrior knights who swore allegiance to the nobles.

18/Sex and the Outer Planets

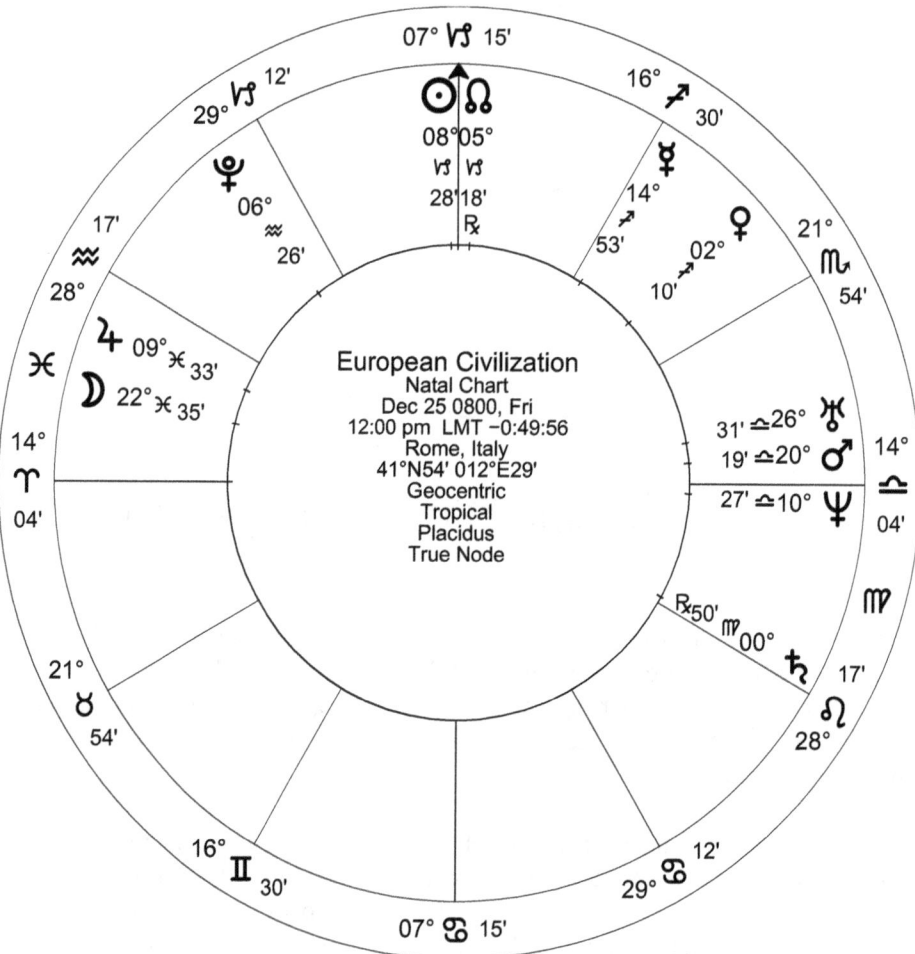

Below them were the masses of serfs who were bound to the soil. There was no middle class. Most artisans were serfs. The clergy formed a separate, autonomous, self-governing body under the control of the Papacy. They owed allegiance to no mundane king or lord. They had their own lands, their own laws, their own economies. They were exempt from all obligations to any temporal state. They paid no taxes, were not required to serve in any army, could not be tried in any civil court, and were not required to obey any secular law that went against their own canon law.

The temporal, civil, secular state, headed by the emperor, was under the domination of Saturn. The spiritual, clerical, Christian domain, headed by the Pope, was under the domination of Jupiter. In this foundation chart for European civilization, these two planets pull against each other in an opposition, with Jupiter the stronger of the two. The agreement between Church and State, which the coronation sealed so amiably for the apparent advantage of both, gradually became the source of almost constant war, diplomatic dissension, and tyranny. From the time of Charlemagne, who gave the people he conquered the choice of death or conversion to Christianity, to the time of Napoleon, who flouted the Pope and replaced the Canon law with his own code, scarcely a day passed without someone being slaughtered in the name of Christ.

By 1100 AD, the papacy had developed a secret police, which for six centuries was the scourge and terror of Europe. Open religious war broke out in the thirteenth century, when Simon de Montfort, fighting for the papacy, annihilated the Albigensians and made a desert of Toulouse and Languedoc. It continued sporadically until the eighteenth century.

Even wars that were not openly religious took on religious overtones, as when, during the Hundred Years War, the English burned the charismatic French leader Joan of Arc as a heretic and a witch.

After the crusades, which were a tremendous cultural shock to the European barbarians, a middle class began to arise in Europe. Under feudal law, a caste of bankers, traders, and artisans had no rights. Yet, because of the increasing need for money by both kings and the papacy to pursue their endless warfare, this new bourgeoisie was cultivated by both sides. Unfortunately, neither the kings nor the popes had any intention of paying back a debt, so the life of the lender was put in jeopardy the moment he pressed for payment. This situation resulted in middle class people banding together and establishing walled cities under the mandates of noblemen who guaranteed to protect them. The bourgeois cities set up their own governments, which tended to be more tolerant and democratic than the feudal governments that prevailed in the countryside.

These cities became havens for a new kind of man, the scientist; and a new activity, the investigation of the physical world to try to discover how it worked. This new activity, as well as the revolutions in thought and in the organization of society to which it led, were governed by Uranus, the first of the outer planets beyond Saturn.

In the development of all civilizations, a middle class of traders, artisans, and professional men eventually arises. Traditionally, this class is ruled by Mercury, the god of commerce. But in the foundation chart of Europe, the bourgeoisie is ruled by the new planet, Uranus. This planet's mode of action is most peculiar. One of the things it symbolizes is *reorganization*. Unlike Saturn, the organizer, it does not operate through normal channels to bring order into the material at hand. Uranus disrupts the normal channels of traditional organization; it destroys the material at hand with sudden, unexplained violence. Without warning, it disrupts every element of the status quo through rebellion and revolutionary ideas, leaving a shambles of disorder behind it. Then, while men are still surveying the ruins like the stunned survivors of an earthquake, Uranus begins its reorganization. Because the Uranian destruction of the old order is so absolute, little of it can be salvaged in viable form. Therefore what emerges in the Uranian reorganization is something new; some system, viewpoint, or way of doing things that men might never have tried if enough of the old order had survived to patch together another Saturnian organization from the pieces.

Whether a middle class is controlled by Mercury, by Uranus, or by both, certain characteristics distinguish it from other classes. It usually comes into being and gains its early wealth by doing jobs and giving services that no one else can, or wants to, do. It creates trading centers, which soon become cities, and it quickly develops the live-and-let-live urban psychology, so necessary for successful trading. It becomes tolerant of new ideas because they may be profitable. It encourages literacy because reading, writing, and figuring are necessary to the conduct of trade. In the interests of trade, its members travel and bring home foreign goods and ideas. It eventually revolts against both the traditional codes of the clergy and the aristocratic privileges of the nobility. If the bourgeoisie win this war, they set up a democratic or pseudo-democratic form of government based on money. Then they begin to produce large numbers of educated professional people; lawyers, doctors, bankers, writers, scientists, teachers, philosophers, and inventors. Gradually, through the efforts of these professional people, the bourgeoisie comes to control the national economy, the courts, the educational system, and the *ideas* of the nation. While all this is happening, the serfs and slaves remain illiterate; and so, to an amazing extent, does the aristocracy, which continues to let the clerics do its reading and writing while it engages in its ancient function of making war.

Usually, the middle class culture doesn't reach beyond the level of mercurial intelligence. In Europe, however, it did, because in the European chart Uranus is almost equal in power to the Sun and is, in some ways, more powerful. Although the Sun is elevated at the Midheaven, it is in the dogmatic sign Capricorn, and it forms no close favorable aspects except a sextile to Jupiter. This describes the alliance between the kings and the Church. But the Sun also makes a close square to Neptune, the planet of subversion. Neptune rules Pisces, the sign symbolic of Christianity; it disposes of Jupiter in that sign, and is in a quincunx aspect of death and suffering to it. This means that as middle class people entered the priesthood, they began to subvert the very foundations of the Church. They did this quite unconsciously (Neptune), through a desire to liberalize its ideas, modernize them, and to make the Church more receptive to the new scientific thought that had entered Europe during the crusades. All these were Uranian efforts at reformation.

Most of the priests and early scientists who rebelled against the Church were of middle class origin. Among them were Roger Bacon, William of Occam, Hus, Luther, Zwingli, Savonrola, the leaders of the Albigensian Crusade, Copernicus, Galileo, Kepler, Tycho Brahe, Giordono Bruno, and many others. They were rewarded by excommunication, imprisonment, and death at the stake. In the long war of ideas the people of Europe endured centuries of suffering (Moon in Pisces in the twelfth house of persecution) at the hands of the Church (Jupiter) and the Inquisition (Neptune).

But the new Uranian ideas would not die. The bourgeoisie continued to cultivate them to see if profit could not be made from them. The bourgeois dictators of the Italian city-states sheltered heretics and financed their inventions, in the hope that sensational new weapons would help them conquer Italy. Protestant Holland, England, and Germany did the same. As the Renaissance progressed, Uranian ideas rolled over Europe from Italy to England, like a great earthquake knocking out the foundations from under every belief men had always held sacred. The Earth ceased to be flat, ceased to be the center of the universe, and began to revolve around the Sun like any other planet. Men went forth to discover new worlds (Uranus). They started using paper, printing presses, steam engines, all sorts of crude industrial machinery, and gun powder.

In this European chart, Uranus is in its most rational and least hysterical position, its ninth house sign, Libra. It falls in the seventh house of war, rebellion, and public enemies, so the new ideas were immediately recognized as "heretical," dangerous to all established interests. This Uranus conjoins Mars (open warfare and violence). And Mars in Europe's chart rules the Ascendant, which in all mundane horoscopes symbolizes the people. As the new ideas circulated (Uranus) among the people through the heretical writings (Uranus) of the scientists and Protestants, it began to occur to a great many ordinary, oppressed people that if kings could take up arms against popes and depose them, they might take up arms against kings with the same happy result. Allover Europe a new breed of political philosopher (Uranus) was urging the people to fight (Mars), for freedom (Uranus), in the name of justice (Libra).

Finally, shortly after the discovery of Uranus, they did. The first European-style civil war broke out in the French Revolution. It set the pattern for all those that were to follow it. It began with the cry, "Liberty, Equality, Fraternity." It created anarchy, moved on to a reign of terror, and ended in dictatorship.

The reason for this is not in Uranus itself, although in certain signs and with certain aspects that planet can become dogmatic and dictatorial. The American Revolution was also a Uranian one, and it did not follow this pattern. The reason Uranian revolutions in Europe end in reigns of terror and dictatorship is that Uranus in Europe's chart disposes of Pluto, symbolic of dictators, and Pluto is in trine aspect to Neptune, symbolic of subversion and of the secret police state. European dictators always have before them the perfect model of a well-organized secret police invented by their own civilization: the Inquisition. When you compare Hitler's methods with St. Dominic's, it is hard to believe that the chart for the Coronation of Charlemagne on Christmas Day, 800, does not still control the destinies of Europe.

There is another thing that has not changed: the European attitude toward sex. As the Mars-Uranus conjunction in the seventh house kept Europe almost continually at war, the sober Jupiter-Saturn order of society continually broke down, resulting in periods of anarchy. In all such periods, sexual taboos go overboard and all who can afford the luxury become openly licentious. In some societies, this results in a change in the status of women and in society's estimate of the role they should play. It did in Russia after the Communist Revolution. But this never happened in Europe.

Mars, ruling the male sex drive, is free of oppression from Saturn and Jupiter, but it is conjunction violent, cold-hearted Uranus, and it is in detriment in the sign Libra. Frequently, Mars in Libra has an inferiority complex about its sexual prowess and must try continuously to prove its virility, not unlike Don Juan. Placed in the seventh house of enemies, in close conjunction with Uranus, the European ideal of maleness is the sexual predator. He must keep women in their place as chattels to prove his power over them.

Venus, the female sex principle, is squared by both Saturn and Jupiter. She is placed in the eighth house of sex in the sexually shallow sign Sagittarius. Thus, she becomes the legitimate prey of the sexual predator. She must either be a whore, a wifely chattel, or a virgin; but in all cases she is regarded with contempt as a thing of no consequence. The square of Saturn to Venus is an aspect that gives social sanction to prostitution. It brings pressure through necessity upon the woman to sell herself for money or status, and sometimes for survival. Throughout most of Europe's history, marriage has been legalized prostitution, because the woman was sold to gain some advantage for herself or her family.

The square of Venus from Jupiter indicates the legality of the process, sanctioned by the Church. It also indicates the disgrace and legalized suffering that may be imposed upon her if she transgresses the code because Jupiter operates from the twelfth house of punishment and from Pisces, the sign of sorrow.

The Moon is the symbol of women as wives and mothers. It is most unfortunate in this chart; for it is in Pisces, sign of bondage, in the twelfth house of bondage. It throws a double quincunx aspect (death and peril) to the Mars-Uranus conjunction in the seventh house of marriage.

The Sun rules the male as husband and father. Here it is at the top of the chart, supreme in authority, it is in the coldly lascivious sign of Capricorn and square Neptune (perversion). Throughout the centuries that this chart has ruled Europe, nothing has created more human misery than the crimes committed in European marriage beds with the bland sanction of both Church and State. As long as this chart continues to rule Europe, the male, the female, and the social attitudes of the civilization toward sex will not change. Women will find only temporary relief from their oppressive roles during periods of anarchy. But we can count on these to be as frequent in the future as they have always been in the past.

Chapter IV

Sexual Distortion in the Saturn-dominated Chart

Adolf Hitler

Adolf Hitler's chart is dominated by a stationary Saturn at the Midheaven. The connections between his planets and the European Foundation chart (Coronation of Charlemagne) explain why he was able to conquer the continent that comes under the dominion of that horoscope. The Spanish ruler Franco gave him token allegiance, but little real help, and Hitler never actually threatened Spain. In spite of all his efforts, he could not conquer Great Britain.

Hitler's dominating Saturn is in exact trine aspect to the Coronation Ascendant, which symbolizes the people of Europe. They believed that they were helpless to resist him. Perhaps the majority secretly admired him and foolishly believed that it was better to submit and live than to try to resist him and die. The trine aspect is peaceable, easy-going, and operates on the line of least resistance. It is seductive. Through threats, persuasion, and lies, Hitler seduced Europe into believing it could not defend itself.

His Jupiter-Moon conjunction in Capricorn falls on the Sun and Midheaven of the Coronation chart. With the greatest ease he took over the governments of Europe, one after another, and imposed his rigid Saturnian order and new code of Nazi laws (Jupiter) upon them.

His Neptune (subversion, propaganda, lies, secret police, prisons, and legalized torture) is within minutes of an exact square to the Coronation Saturn. The European governments by that time were mostly inefficient, unstable bureaucracies (Saturn retrograde in Virgo in the sixth

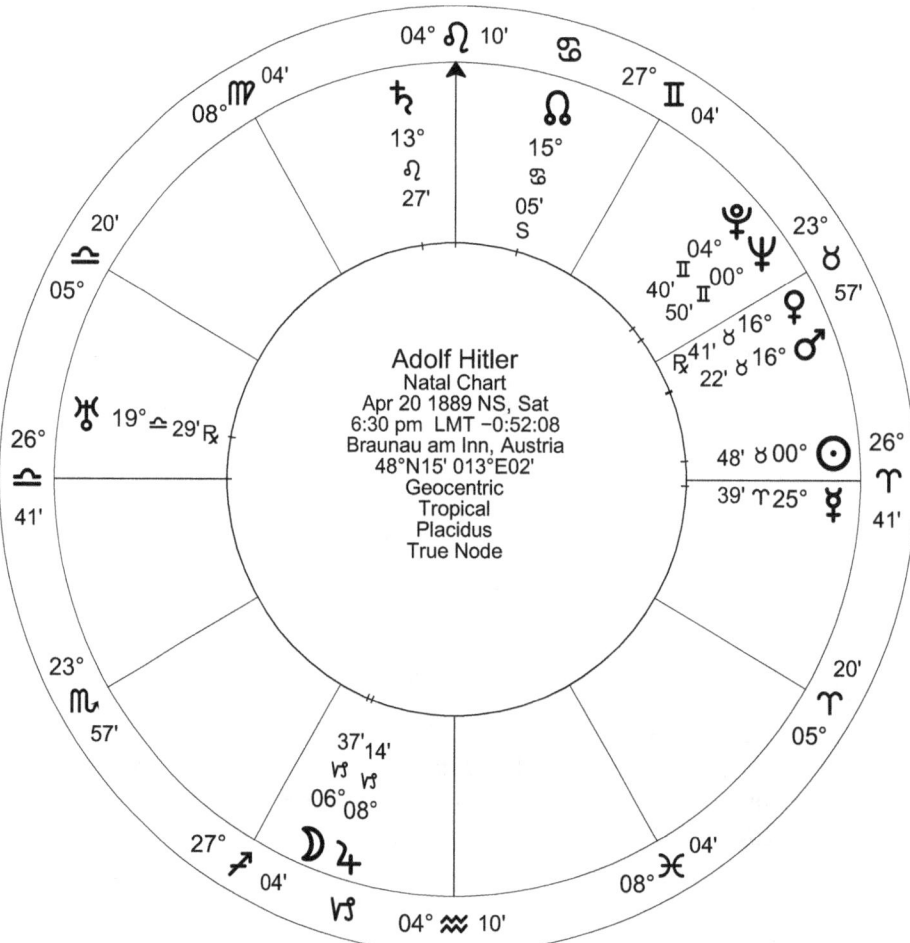

house, the sign of bureaucracy) that betrayed (Neptune) the people to Hitler. Only two Continental kings, Denmark and Norway, whose countries lay outside the Holy Roman Empire, behaved royally and tried to set an example of courage to the people they were powerless to defend. However, because this aspect is a square (struggle, resistance, conflict) it eventually operated to Hitler's detriment. The people of every conquered country set up underground units to sabotage the Nazis. This is Neptune's way of fighting, and it demanded great courage, for everyone who undertook it risked imprisonment, torture, and death in Hitler's terrible Neptunian camps. Much of this activity was fostered and directed by Communists in the conquered countries (Neptune symbolizes Communism).

Hitler's Sun, however, is in exactly as close a trine to the Coronation Saturn as his Neptune is square it. This made it easy for him to seduce government officials and gain their cooperation.

He seduced them into believing they would be rewarded (Sun trine Saturn) by the New Order if they helped him.

In my observation, the Sun square Saturn is the strongest of all aspects in adversity and will undertake to struggle against the most overwhelming odds with courage and dogged perseverance. It is an aspect of people and nations that raise themselves up far beyond the station they were born in through their own efforts. Hitler himself had this aspect, though, with very wide orbs. But the *trine* between the Sun and Saturn is lax in self-discipline and wants to make it the easy way. People and nations with this aspect can usually be bought off with promises of personal material gains, or with bribes. Their principles are weaker than their greed, and they are often content to be satellites if their subordination will buy them security. This is especially true if the aspect occurs in earth signs, as here.

Hitler's Neptune-Pluto conjunction falls in opposition to the Venus of the Coronation chart. Pluto rules the genes and sex as a primordial biological urge. The race laws of Hitler's New Order were a weirdly aberrant pressure upon the female sex principle, because while the Nazi sex laws destroyed the Jupiter-Saturn code of sexual morality, as determined by the Coronation chart, women were in an even position than before. An interesting feature of Hitler's sex laws was that women were encouraged to have illegitimate children with "Aryan" men, and were rewarded for it. Under the sexual code of the Coronation chart, they had been disgraced and punished for producing bastards, who in turn were disgraced and punished for being bastards. Neptune rules illegitimate children.

Finally, Hitler's rising Uranus falls on the seventh house Mars (war) of the Coronation chart. Even though no country ruled by the Coronation chart put up a fight against him, Hitler brought violent death, destruction, devastation, and revolution to the whole of Charlemagne's Europe.

There is very little authentic information about Hitler's sex life or sexual orientation. We know that many women found him magnetically attractive. At least one, and possibly more, committed suicide because of him. He kept a mistress, Eva Braun, for many years and finally married her just before he himself committed suicide. He had acute paranoid delusions of persecution, which according to Freudian psychological theory, always indicate latent or repressed homosexuality. He was extremely fearful that someone might shoot him (Mars conjunction his ruler Venus, both square Saturn). For this reason he wore bullet-proof armor under his clothes, and had all the linden trees cut down on Unter-den-Linden so that no one could hide in the dense foliage and shoot him on one of his public appearances. He condoned—even encouraged—homosexuality among his storm troopers, the Hitler youth, the Gestapo, and his elite SS. This was not actually a break with German tradition, as homosexuality had been tacitly accepted and was common among the Prussian military elite of the imperial regime. But at least attempts were made to keep it secret. Under the Nazis, homosexuality was considered a nobler form of sexual expression than heterosexuality. Finally, Hitler was a sadist: he made torture the basis of his judicial system; he ordered the extermination of the Jews, and when they were gone he planned to proceed to the extermination of all other non-Aryans-Slavs, Greeks, Italians, and Frenchmen of the Mediterranean type. For his private amusement, he had films made of the Gestapo torture chambers, which he would then view in his hideouts and sometimes even show at the select parties he gave for the privileged few.

In short, he was a sexually motivated monster. If he had not been able to "sublimate" his perverse sex drives in politics, through which he hoped to fulfill his sadistic ambition to bring the whole world under his boots, he probably would have been a murderer of the slasher-ripper type. I often wonder what his personal astrologers were able to tell him that would flatter him enough to assure the preservation of their lives a little longer. Evidently, most of them lapsed into an honesty he found unwelcome, for sooner or later he had them killed or imprisoned, and he outlawed astrology in his domains.

In the United States during World War II, this horoscope of Hitler was probably more carefully studied and more often reproduced than any other chart. Yet I do not remember ever reading an analysis of it that penetrated to the warped sexual motivations behind his career or grasped the essentially psychopathic nature of the man. Perhaps, everyone was more interested in trying to discover when the world would finally be rid of him.

The Saturn-dominated chart is puritanical. All the normal functions of the inner planets, when they are distorted by Saturnian domination, appear to be sinful. They must be repressed or twisted into forms of expression unnatural to them but pleasing to Saturn.

The inner planets are the ones through which we assert the fact that we are human beings. Every principle and activity they symbolize is essential to the development and preservation of the individual and the species. The will to survive and create (the Sun); the emotional need for sympathy and understanding that makes us found families and societies (the Moon); the need to communicate through which we preserve knowledge and pass it on (Mercury); the aggressive energy or male sex principle (Mars) through which we defend ourselves and act outward to control our environment; the social instinct or female sex principle (Venus) through which we order our environment and balance our desires against the needs and rights of others. And finally, the absolute necessity to assure the survival of the human race through the heterosexual sex act—cooperation between Mars and Venus.

To make a human being feel that any of these natural expressions are sinful and that he should feel guilty if he longs to fulfill any of them requires rigorous social pressure. It is the nature of Saturn to bring that pressure, to force our human instincts into bondage to society, to transform us into social robots. In a chart like Hitler's, which is overwhelmed by the power of Saturn, the individual feels a terrible sense of guilt for every natural impulse he does not repress or distort into something he cannot recognize as a natural instinct. Every success he achieves in this direction makes him increasingly proud of himself. And with some justification, because with each severe repression he has become a little more inhuman; and there is really nothing more difficult for a human being to do than to achieve a high degree of inhumanity. This pride in the repression of one's humanity is the source of the typical Saturnian megalomania and delusions of grandeur, of Saturnian dogmatism and intolerance of all merely "human" weaknesses, and of the Saturnian conviction that *my* outstanding success in repressing *my* humanity gives me the absolute right to force *you* to repress yours.

Individuals and societies who submit whole-heartedly to the domination of Saturn can achieve great things. Unfortunately, Saturn does no favors. For everything he seems to give, he exacts full price, with interest if you bought on the time-payment plan. Initially, human beings adjust to Saturn's demands by cultivating a sense of guilt and shame because they are human. Saturn rewards them with a little money, an increase in status, or some worldly power. Proud of his gains, the individual decides that what he gave for them was a trifle compared to what he got; so he makes a few more concessions to Saturn and again is suitably rewarded with worldly goods and power. As this process continues, however, the nature that made him begins to take subtle vengeance upon him for rejecting her. Unconsciously, he begins to feel guilt and shame not for being human, but for rejecting his humanity. He becomes incapable of love, incapable of normal sex, incapable of communicating honestly with others, and emotionally starved. He becomes a non-person. He begins to feel terribly insecure, panic-stricken, at the manifestation of anything that reminds him of humanity or human beings. The horrible suspicion arises in him that in spite of all he has, human beings have something he lacks. In mounting terror, he begins to fear that whatever it is, it makes them more powerful than he is and endangers his existence.

Then, the compulsion to justify himself sets in. He begins to withdraw from the human beings who seem to threaten him. As he loses contact with them, he loses touch with reality and begins to distort it. People must be made to fear, envy and obey him. As he is a robot in the service of Saturn, they must be made over into robots in his service, eternally singing his praises. He demands an increasing toll of human sacrifices so that he himself may continue to feel alive. He receives the revelation that he is the chosen vessel through which a mighty, supernatural force will realize itself and reform the world. He begins to hear voices from the supernatural force, directing his actions. It is a great relief to hear them because they prove that he is no longer responsible for what he does.

Both Goethe and Spengler maintained that one particular myth expressed the essence and meaning of Europe. Hitler's life and psychological development were the living embodiment of that myth: the story of Faust, the man who sold his soul to the Devil.

His chart describes the step-by-step progress toward inhumanity. (For him, the initial acts were easier than for most because no planet falls in a water sign. In astrology, each element symbolizes a value essential to human life. When one element is lacking (has no representation through a planet or the Ascendant) the individual is born without innate, unconscious understanding of that value. But, since it is essential to life, he must compensate for the lack through the other values (elements) that are represented. Compensation is not replacement, however. It is a diversion by art or force of something from a channel where it belongs into channels foreign to it. It is like diverting the waters of a river to irrigate a desert. Our food supply is assured as long as the irrigation system works, but to maintain it demands constant vigilance and careful controls, as the original river did not. Those who live by the river feel secure in the enjoyment of its benefits. Those who depend on the irrigation system do not: at any moment something may happen to destroy their work, and they will starve.

Any chart that lacks an element is unbalanced in a most fundamental way. Experience has demonstrated that this is not always bad, although it probably always results in more than usually painful experiences for the individual, and in greater than usual problems in adjusting to the society. In the majority of cases, the compensations are constructive.

Some elements are easier to compensate for than others. Lack of air (intellect) may be replaced by great emotional insight and result in artistic or musical genius. Lack of earth (material resources) may be compensated for by great spiritual insight (fire), and so create a mystic or a philosopher. Lack of fire may be compensated for by great intellectual development that results in scientific breakthroughs, new codes of laws, or revolutionary political theories. But it is very hard to compensate for the lack of water, symbolizing our emotions and our emotional values.

Usually, compensation takes place through the element most heavily represented in the chart. In Hitler's case, this was earth. It is impossible to compensate for the inability to feel like a human being with material resources and the attainment of power over other human beings. The attempt to do so results in the most intense psychic insecurity.

Hitler's great charismatic appeal to the German people and the undeniable personal magnetism he exerted over those who knew him came from the Moon-Jupiter conjunction, both trine the Sun. This conjunction falls at the midpoint between his Sun and the Mars-Venus conjunction, so it also affected those two planets. This is a lucky configuration because it inspires confidence and trust in others. But because the aspect occurs between the inner planets, the confidence and trust extended only to Hitler's own tribe, to people like himself—the Germans. The domination of this pleasant configuration by the tenth-house Saturn inspired loathing and distrust among outsiders. Hitler longed to seduce the English, who he felt were natural allies of the Germans, and he could never understand why, in spite of all his charm and magnetism, he failed.

He channeled his lack of emotional understanding through this configuration. Through it, he made himself appear highly emotional, although, in fact, he was hysterical. Hysteria is often the result of trying to channel water values through earth values. The insecurity of the replacement inspires panic. This conditioning underlay all his reactions to the outside world. The measures he took to increase his own safety grew more and more desperate. But no matter what he did, his inner panic grew worse. Toward the end of his life, the tension became unbearable, he lost all rational judgment, and his actions were patently insane.

One feature of Hitler's chart that had profound political significance was the close pairing of eight of the ten planets: Moon-Jupiter, Mercury-Sun, Mars-Venus, and Neptune-Pluto. Such pairing is the signature of the opportunist. One cannot read a history of the period without being impressed by the apparently masterful way Hitler took advantage of every personal and historical circumstance to promote himself and achieve his goals. Historians often assume and sometimes state that if the times had been different, if Germany had not been in such economic and political chaos between the wars, Hitler could not have risen to power. I do not believe this is true. He took advantage of the circumstances that existed, certainly. But if they had been different, he still would have taken advantage of them. He molded his personality and directed his actions to fit the times, which were grotesque, exactly as if he had been a tailor cutting a suit to fit a misshapen man. He made such a good job of it because his earth trine endowed him with an amazingly acute perception of exactly what the opportunities were within the familiar orbit of Germany and Europe. Beyond that orbit, he had no perception of opportunity. His famous intuition failed him completely in every judgment he made of how England, America, and Russia would behave in relation to himself. He had cut his cloth to the wrong pattern for them. This is a common fate of opportunists.

However, if the times had been calm and constructive in his own orbit, I believe he would have molded himself to fit them and still would have risen to power. The only difference might have been that he would not have had to make such a clown of himself to take advantage of them.

Hitler's personal sex problems began early in his life with his relations to his father, whom he despised. People born with Jupiter in Capricorn always seem able to find reasons for disliking their fathers.

Sometimes, the feeling is subjective and unwarranted, but frequently it is not. Among my clientele, I have had many cases where Jupiter in Capricorn indicated definite character defects in the father that warped the development of the child, although other children in the family who did not have Jupiter in this position were not affected adversely. If the character defect is real and not merely imagined by the child, it does not seem to matter exactly what it consists of. The father may have been an alcoholic, a woman chaser, a gambling spendthrift, an irresponsible bum, a weakling incapable of earning a living, a cruel tyrant, someone the child never knew, or someone who abandoned the child at an early age. In one case in my files, the father was a man of talent and ability, but he died when the child was six years old. The child grew up *blaming* the father for dying, as if he had done it on purpose, deliberately abandoning the boy, deliberately making his mother suffer, and placing great burdens on her. If it happens that the mother dies and the father raises the children in a kind, responsible way, the Jupiter-in-Capricorn child usually blames the father for the mother's death.

It seems to be a position where the father can't win, no matter what he is or does. The child's psychic relations with him are uncomfortable, uncharitable, or contemptuous. Hitler felt that his father was a worthless, ineffectual weakling—a frightened little civil servant who trembled at the whisper of authority. Usually, a boy's opinion of his father, formed in childhood, becomes his subconscious opinion of all males as he grows up. Hitler was no exception to the rule. First he held all Austrian males in contempt because his father was Austrian: like him, they must all be silly weaklings, grubbing for a living, shaking in fright of every bully who came along. When Germany lost the First World War, he enlarged his contempt to include all German males. When the French let him take the Ruhr with scarcely a protest and Chamberlain at Munich handed him Czechoslovakia, he included all European males. Since the Jews were not warlike, the Russians and Poles were Slavs, and the Americans were mere moneygrubbers, he'd never had anything but contempt for any of them to begin with. It's no wonder he believed that a boundless opportunity existed to make the Germans over into a race of heroes who would never meet resistance as they trampled the rest of the world into the mud beneath their boots.

This contempt for males lies at the root of Hitler's suspected homosexuality. A client of mine who through the years has become a close friend made a very acute observation once. He said, "Homosexuals don't hate women. They hate men. The whole homosexual relationship is an insult to masculine integrity." He should know. He was born with Jupiter in Capricorn, lived through the experience of feeling contempt for his father, became a homosexual, finally learned to accept himself in that role only to discover that it really was merely a role for him. He is now in the process of growing up into heterosexuality. By profession he is a psychologist.

I believe that Hitler's first heterosexual experience was incestuous, with a sister or cousin; probably he experimented with both. I would time the overt phase of the relationship at about age fifteen, when his Sun, by solar arc, came to the conjunction with his Mars-Venus conjunction. Masturbatory experience with girls in the family may have begun earlier, at twelve, when his Sun squared the natal Saturn and his Moon, also by solar arc, squared his Uranus. This is an astrological judgment. I have been unable to find any data about his early sexual life.

If my judgment is correct, he was undoubtedly aware of the "illegality" of his activity, and the loathing the mere idea of incest inspired in the Church, the State, and the people he knew. Because of the easy trine made by his inner planets, however, he would have had no difficulty in overcoming the scruples of his female relatives, and the ease of his conquests would have convinced him there was nothing really wrong in what he was doing. It would have been a surface conviction that merely glossed over all the sin and damnation mythology he had undoubtedly been taught, like all the other children of the late nineteenth century. With his dominating Saturn, Hitler's sense of guilt and fear of punishment could never be repressed very far below the surface of his consciousness.

As the Sun passed its conjunction to Venus, he probably gave up the relationship, and when it moved into the quincunx aspect (150°) to Uranus, he probably tried heterosexual relations with a woman not related to him—someone with whom he was deeply infatuated. I believe this was a disaster that left him in doubt of his virility. I think that he then imagined that he was being punished for having allowed his female relatives to seduce him. This is the "knife-in the-back" psychological syndrome that he later used to excuse Germany's defeat in the war and the role he claimed the Jews played in it.

If such an event did occur on the quincunx aspect of the Sun to Uranus, it would have inspired the greatest anxiety in him and made him feel that something was wrong with him. By committing a terrible sin (incest), he had brought about a terrible punishment (impotence), which deprived him of his masculinity and made him an ineffectual weakling like his father. The world might not know it, but *he* knew it. All his efforts in the future must be bent to keep anyone from ever finding out what he was really like. To prove his virility, he must take every opportunity to stamp out weaklings like his father (himself).

This astrological reading explains a great deal about Hitler's character: his homosexuality, his hero-worship of the Teutonic knights, his sadism, his anti-Semitism, his compulsion to legalize both his own criminal actions and those of the Nazi State. To assuage his own guilt, everything had to be made to look justified, legal, official—from the burning of the Reichstag to the occupation of the Ruhr to the Munich conference to the invasion of Poland.

It also shed light on the motives underlying some of his actions, which—at least to me—were never satisfactorily explained. One of these was the murder of Röhm and his bodyguard during the "Night of the Long Knives." Nothing I have read indicates to me that Rohm was other than loyal to Hitler or that Röhm had any intention of betraying him. I believe, however, that Röhm and Hitler were lovers of long standing, and that after Hitler was made Reichschancellor and took absolute control of Germany he began to worry that Röhm might be in a position to blackmail him. So, as soon as he felt powerful enough to do so, Hitler had his friend killed on the trumped up charge that he was plotting treason.

Most of Hitler's warped rationalizations and evil adjustments to his psychological and sexual problems were worked out through the Venus-Mars conjunction square Saturn. Because of the angular position of these planets, he repeatedly acted out his aberrations in public arenas that finally enlarged to include the world.

Besides impotence, homosexuality, sadism, and violence, this aspect did something else for Hitler: it made him a pyromaniac. From the time he had been a soldier, the fiery bombardments of the war had fascinated him. After Germany was defeated, he felt he was their innocent victim. (He was wounded in the war.) Once he summoned up the courage to set fire to the Reichstag and got by with it successfully, things changed. He developed a passion for setting unquenchable fires—a will to Götterdämmerung. The fires got bigger and bigger, but nothing appeased him until finally he himself died in the biggest of them all.

The Marquis de Sade

The Marquis de Sade was another person with a Saturn-dominated chart who suffered from extreme sexual aberrations. His horoscope is included here because of its historical interest and because it has many points of resemblance to Hitler's.

De Sade was born June 2, 1740, in Paris. The hour of birth is unknown, so this chart is cast by the Johndro method for the place of birth. (An explanation of this method is given in Appendix A.)

Like Hitler, de Sade had Venus and Mars adversely involved with his tenth-house Saturn. Unlike Hitler, he married young, at age twenty-three, when his Neptune (symbol of perversion) came by solar arc direction to a conjunction with his Venus. Undoubtedly, the marriage was arranged by his family and was the last thing he would have undertaken of his own freewill. De Sade's homosexuality was not repressed. I judge, from the square of the Moon to the Sun-Jupiter conjunction and its trine to Uranus, that he had given it free reign from childhood, and that his preference for male lovers was well known to him and to everyone else by the time he was twenty-three.

Nevertheless, his marriage must have been a great psychological strain on him. Many overt homosexuals assume that they can have heterosexual relations *if they wish*, and of course, some can. Probably de Sade was one who couldn't. If so, his impotence with his wife must have infuriated him. Like Hitler, he must have equated impotence in a normal situation with lack of masculinity and hence with lack of power. Hitler, with his Mars-Venus conjunction in Taurus square Saturn in Leo had to prove his virility by securing all the resources of the earth (the fixed signs rule resources). De Sade, with his Venus conjunct Saturn in Cancer square Mars in Aries, had to justify himself in a much more personal, direct way. (The cardinal signs rule our personal reactions to situations and people.) Since a woman had humiliated him, women had to suffer for it. By torturing them (Mars square Saturn and Venus) he proved his superiority over them, avenged his humiliation (Moon square Sun indicates sensitivity to humiliation), and gained sex-

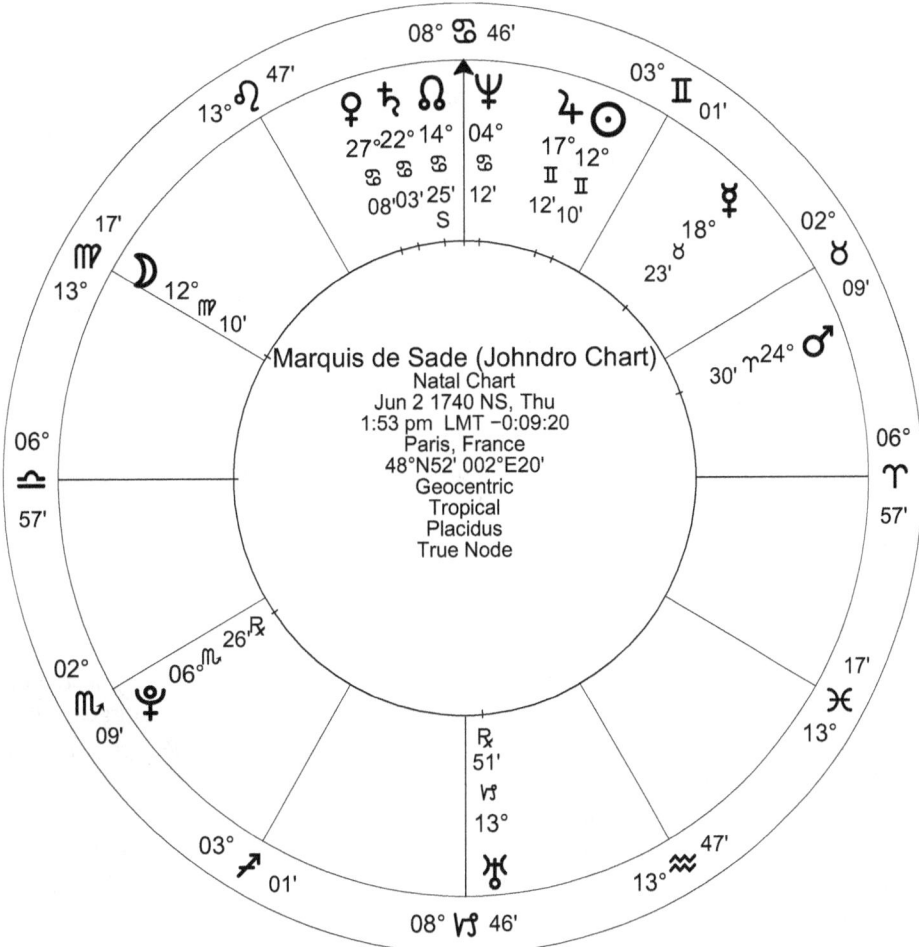

ual satisfaction by abnormal means in which his mind and imagination played a greater role than his actions (Moon in grand trine with Mercury and Uranus).

Within a month of his marriage, he began to frequent a brothel where he committed sadistic excesses that resulted in his imprisonment in October 1763. He was imprisoned again in 1778. The years from 1784 to 1789 he spent in the Bastille, where he amused himself by writing many of the books describing the sexual perversion now known by his name. In keeping with the greater cardinality of his chart, he was much more exhibitionistic than Hitler and much less secretive about his personal involvement with violence. Hitler probably never tortured anyone in person. On the contrary, he was personally squeamish and suffered from an almost maidenly sense of modesty. De Sade enjoyed shocking people, as is often the case with an angular Mars in Aries, badly afflicted.

When the mob released him from the Bastille, he became politically involved with the Revolution, as one might expect from his tenth-house Saturn and the Uranus-Neptune opposition across the meridian. The shock value of his writings on sex has obscured the fact that he also wrote books on politics and sociology. He was still unable to stay out of jail, however. The Commune found him too moderate for their taste and had him imprisoned for political heresy. When he was released, he found that he had been bankrupted by the Revolution. (Pluto, ruler of his second house of money had progressed to orb of opposition to his Neptune, symbol of bankruptcy.) He managed to eke out a living by writing and producing plays at Versailles. Mars in Aries is always the entrepreneur, while Venus in the tenth house gravitates to occupations that amuse or adorn the public whenever it has to earn a living.

By 1801, Pluto, symbol of dictatorship, came within orb of opposition to his Midheaven, symbol of the authority of the State. He foolishly published some political tracts attacking Napoleon and Josephine. He was arrested again. But this time the court, examining his long record of sexual crimes, decided he was insane and committed him to the asylum of Charenton, where he died on December 2, 1814, at the age of seventy-three years and six months. At that time, Saturn was coming into conjunction with his natal (Johndro) Ascendant and Pluto had moved into opposition to his natal Saturn, by one degree direction.

An interesting feature of his chart is that his wife had children, but I judge they were not his, although he claimed them. Aquarius, ruling his fifth house of children suggests they were adopted. Uranus, lord of Aquarius, is retrograde in its twelfth-house sign, Capricorn, indicating that there were suppressed or hidden facts about them. Uranus symbolizes adoption, and it is opposing Neptune, symbol of illegitimacy. But as far as the world was concerned (and his reputation for potency), he got by with the deception because Uranus was in a grand trine with Mercury and the Moon. No doubt long before he died he had convinced himself that he had really begotten them.

Like Hitler, he was a great liar. De Sade's lies were a necessary defense against his own self-hatred. While there is no doubt that de Sade actually committed the sex crimes of which he was accused, and there is strong evidence that some women may have died as a result of them, most of what he wrote in his books and claimed to have done is pure fiction. Nevertheless, it is only because of his books that the world remembers him at all. They describe a complex syndrome of sexual aberration that had gone unnamed until it became associated with him.

Chapter V

Sexual Distortion in the Jupiter-dominated Chart

Sigmund Freud was the father of the sexual revolution. He was born May 6, 1856, just ten years after the discovery of the planet Neptune, in Freiburg, Moravia (Poland).

It is a map of great constructive power, with its energy—genius, if you like—channeled through the square between Saturn and Jupiter. These two planets are 88 degrees and only slightly more than two houses apart. Freud's ambition was boundless, he worked doggedly to promote himself and his ideas—often against serious opposition from the conservative (Saturn) medical profession—and he was just as neurotic as some of his patients.

Like Hitler and de Sade, Freud had Mars square Saturn, yet he was neither a sadist nor a homosexual, and he abhorred violence. Why did the aspect operate so differently for him?

In the first place, although the orbs are close enough, the aspect is formed out of sign, with the retrograde Mars in Libra and Saturn in Gemini. The air element may be extremely aggressive intellectually, as Freud was, but it is not particularly violent. One who has the aspect in air is more apt to engage in verbal fights than in physical ones, and to be the victim of violence rather than its perpetuator. Freud made many enemies and engaged in controversies both to defend his ideas and to humiliate those who disagreed with him. Mars square Saturn is a paranoid aspect: people who have it often feel persecuted, beset by enemies, and fearful of loss of status. When the aspect severely afflicts the inner planets, as it did with Hitler and de Sade, the individual may lash out sadistically to crush his real or imagined enemies.

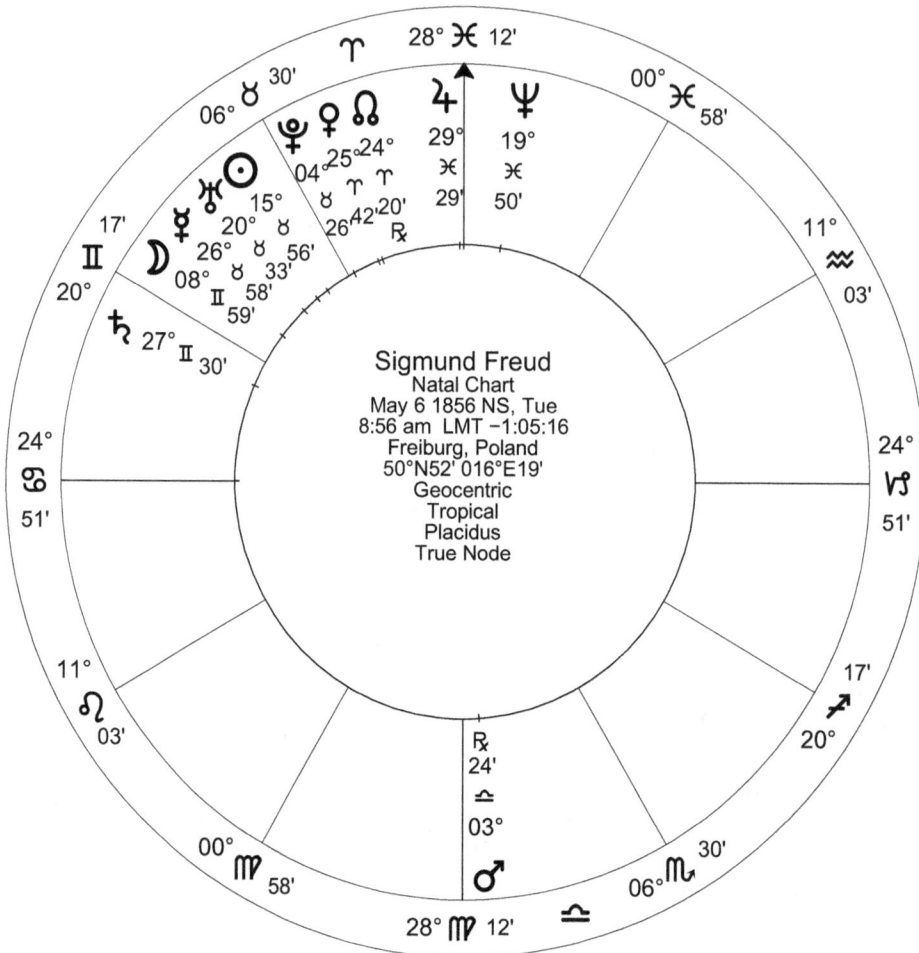

There is no doubt that Freud was hypersensitive to criticism, to the vilification of his ideas, and to the fact that he was a Jew. In his desire to climb to the top, he was sometimes unscrupulous in his treatment of colleagues and pupils. He even stooped, at times, to borrowing their ideas or plagiarizing their work without giving them proper credit. Those who resented such treatment broke off their association with him, yet few of them criticized him publicly for his injustice to them. Most of them felt that he was the great master. He was hard to get along with, dogmatic, and jealous (Mars square Saturn) of other people's achievements—but still, he *had* invented psychoanalysis, the great breakthrough in modern psychology. So no matter what he did, they felt they owed him a great debt.

One of the hidden powers of Freud's chart that made for a constructive use of it, rather than a destructive one, is that neither Venus nor the Moon is in an oppressive relationship with the

Mars-Saturn square. Venus, at 25 Aries, is in a lucky sextile aspect to Saturn and in mutual reception with Mars. To judge the power of a mutual reception, imagine each planet back in its own sign but do not change its degree. If we place Venus at 25 Libra in this case, it acts as if it were trine Saturn. Mars in its true position at 3 Libra is in a trine aspect to both Mercury and the Moon, with the exact focus of the trine at the midpoint between those two planets. When transposed to 3 Aries, the aspect is weakened, becoming a sextile; but at 3 Aries Mars conjoins Jupiter and the Midheaven.

Without this transposition of the mutual reception, Mars is in opposition to Jupiter, forming the third point of a T-square with Saturn. The energy created by a T-square, particularly if it involves Mars, is enormous. It seeks release through the planet on the short end of the T, in this case Saturn. Saturn in any air sign tends to operate as an intellectual force of great sobriety: it takes its ideas seriously. In Gemini, it falls in its own fifth house sign of creativity. Gemini is the sign ruling writing, inventions, and communication. Freud released the energy of the T-square intellectually, through inventing a new psychological theory, which he expressed masterfully in writing of such high quality that, even if we disagree with everything he says, he never bores us. But Freud's Saturn actually falls in his twelfth house of hidden values, secret motivations, and unsolved mysteries. Freud's invention was the discovery of the subconscious mind, ruled by the twelfth house. He conceived it to be the source of man's undoing, the secret enemy of his conscious, rational mind, and a veritable garbage can of perverse desires and wickedness—all of which are twelfth-house values.

A second reason why Freud used his Mars-Saturn square constructively is the opposition between Mars and Jupiter. Charles Carter thought this was absolutely the worst aspect a person could be born with. Then he goes on to say that it is extremely common in the maps of creative artists, writers, dramatists, actors, and musicians. In my own experience, I have found that it is equally common in the maps of research scientists, philosophers, social reformers, and political rebels. It is rare in the charts of the mentally ill and those who commit violent crimes, although the square between Jupiter and Mars is fairly common among such disturbed people.

Creative genius is so rare that we cannot pinpoint any one astrological configuration as responsible for it: our statistical data are too limited. I can only say that one of the aspects commonly found in the charts of unusually talented people who create something tangible with their talent is Mars opposition Jupiter. In many, if not most, of these cases, the value of the work is not recognized until late in the creator's life or after his death. It is work in advance of its time, of such startling originality that the inventor's contemporaries find it "kooky," "ugly," "immoral," impractical, or just plain crazy. They often decide that the person who created it is equally crazy, so they mock and ridicule him and in many cases destroy all of his work they can get their hands on. The writer can't find a publisher, the painter can't get work exhibited, the dramatist can't get it performed, and the inventor can't get it subsidized. Assuming they do, after years of trying, get printed, exhibited, performed, the critics lacerate both the work *and its creator.* They try to make this gifted person the laughing stock of society, a moronic comedian. If too intelligent to fit that role, the immorality label is pinned on the creative genius: he has a mistress, she's a drunkard, he refuses to work for a living, she's an atheist or a political heretic, he's a homosexual, a wife-beater, and corrupter of the young. If, like Freud, this person's life is stodgy beyond belief and filled only with work, then the writing and thinking produced are immoral, corrupting, and obscene.

In the majority of cases, this rejection by society of such people and their life work results in poverty, a profound sense of futility, loneliness, the misery of being social outcasts, and—sometimes—premature death caused by hardship. In a few rare cases, like Richard Wagner's, these individuals finally manage to get hold of enough money to produce their own work. The money is usually lost, but the chances that their works will survive, perhaps long enough to assure final acceptance, are increased. In still fewer cases, like Freud's, the gifted person survives all enemies and lives to be proclaimed an absolute master.

To give an idea of the type of person the aspect helps to produce and the effect it may have on the individual life, here are a few examples: Alexander II of Russia, who freed the serfs; Sarah Bernhardt; Luther Burbank; Mahatma Gandhi; Greta Garbo; John Hazelrigg and Alan Leo, astrologers who labored to bring astrology back from the disrepute into which it had fallen; Fiorello La Guardia; Franz Liszt; David Lloyd George; General Ludendorff; Auguste Lumiere, who invented a process of color photography in 1893; Ramsay MacDonald; H. L. Menoken, Tom Mooney, early labor leader; Friedrich Nietzsche; Robert Peary, the explorer; Cecil Rhodes; Leopold Stokowski; Peter Ilytch Tchaikovsky; Tennyson; Nicola Tesla, the electrical inventor; Sun-Yat-Sen; Swami Vivekananda; Richard Wagner; Mary, Queen of Scots and her enemy, Elizabeth I of England; Cesar Borgia, who tried unsuccessfully to unify Italy; Alphonse Daudet; Maria Bashkirtseff; Sir Thomas More; Isaac Barrow, the great mathematician who was Newton's teacher; Oliver Goldsmith; John Locke, whose political and philosophical ideas were incorporated into the Declaration of Independence and the Constitution; Joseph Priestley, the early chemist who discovered oxygen—a mob burned down his laboratory because he supposedly practiced black magic; Sir William Petty, the first great English economist whose ideas laid the foundation for Adam Smith's work; and Karl Marx.

Certainly, if conformity to the *status quo* is our idea of what makes a happy and prosperous life, it would be well to be born without Mars opposing Jupiter. Obviously, the aspect incites action (Mars) against the accepted moral codes or traditional beliefs (Jupiter) of the times and society. What is so extraordinary, considering that Mars is involved, is that the action taken is seldom violent and almost never criminal. Cesar Borgia, whose chart was violent and criminal because of other configurations, stands out in a list that is predominantly intellectual. These people were pioneers of ideas. They fought traditional dogmas of their times with courage and persistence, at great cost to their security and prestige. They were heretics, fighting the establishment (Jupiter). Because they so often fought alone, they were branded as idealistic fools, quixotic clowns tilting at windmills to no good purpose.

The aspect invites the persecution of society because the person who has it endangers its complacency. When the rest of the chart is powerful, the Mars becomes like a dagger ripping away the veils of hokum that blind us to the silliness—even viciousness—of many of the things we have always taken for granted. The rebellious activity of Mars pitted against Jupiter takes an intellectual form because Jupiter is the law in the most fundamental and broadest sense. It is the whole fabric of traditional codes and beliefs that command our automatic, unthinking obedience. It's whatever has to be true because we have believed it for so long it can't possibly be false. When the codes of morality and custom reach this stage of universal acceptance, they come perilously close to being superstitions.

When Mars is opposition Jupiter, there is a genius for detecting the sacred cow. No matter how Mars is actualized, there is always danger, an enemy who slashes and rips without mercy. Jupiter is a gambler, but no fighter. When one of his superstitions is endangered, he marshals all the satraps of society to save it. If he loses, as he does when genius backs up the fighting Mars, he goes over to the enemy with all flags flying. From the way Western Christian society began to adore Freud after World War I, it's easy to think that sexual repression had never been a sacred cow.

The aspect does seem to confer a strong dramatic sense, even when its possessor has nothing to do with the theatre. For scholars, intellectuals, and reformers, this means that their ideas have strong shock value. They stand out dramatically in opposition to the codified "normal" thought. An aura of sinful glamour adheres to whatever has shock value so that people who had never read Freud or Marx "knew all about" psychoanalysis or Communism because they'd "heard so much about them." The well-publicized heresy fascinates conformists. Whether the heretic wins or loses, the conformist enjoys a vicarious thrill of excitement, which is badly needed to enliven a dull life. Because it is easier for most of us to identify emotionally with a dramatic personality than it is to identify emotionally with dramatic ideas, the shock value of the ideas is gradually transferred to the person who has the ideas and who becomes a devil personified—a candidate for burning. For a few, though, this person becomes a persecuted messiah, a guru, the master who attracts disciples like a magnet.

A few of these people, like Mary Queen of Scots, Wagner, and Gandhi, actually did have dramatic personalities; and, of course, all of the actors with the aspect do, or they could not be successful actors. But many, like Freud, Marx, Mencken, Priestley, or Nietzsche, have quiet personalities and live routine lives dedicated to work. Frequently, they are so retiring—even shy—that they cannot publicize their ideas. Their enemies or disciples with more flamboyant personalities must do it for them.

As with the Sun square Saturn, there is a tendency for people born with Mars opposition Jupiter to rise in station through their own efforts. Some, like Marx, who seem to fall in station during their lives, attain an awesome power after their deaths through the activity of disciples.

The impact of Freud's ideas upon the Western world was devastating. He lived through times of revolution, rapid transition, and anarchy, when one traditional code after another was demolished. But what was destroyed was always quickly replaced by another code, so that some sort of order was rapidly imposed. He saw Darwin's theory of evolution depose Adam and Eve; Communism replace Russian feudalism; dictators replace kings; industrial economies replace the dying agrarian economies. Only the code of Christian sexual morality, which Freud shattered, has been replaced by nothing at all. When he was born, it seemed to be the one code so firmly entrenched as to be impervious to attack. When he died, so little was left of it that no one except the few who continued to live in archaic backwaters of thought knew what his own sexual orientation was, or should be. Where sex was concerned, Freud left everyone on his own in an emotional jungle unregulated by law, custom, morality, or any religion he could respect or fear. True, there were still codes on the books, and people who gave lip service to the codes. But somehow Freud had managed to extract all their teeth.

Freud was born into a world where the first obligation of every right-thinking person was to see to it that his sexual conduct conformed to a rigid set of rules he was taught in his cradle: even his thoughts must conform. The penalties for nonconformity were so severe that any sacrifice or inner pain was preferable to being caught in a non-conforming gesture. The effort people made to hide even normal sexual impulses from themselves and their neighbors was comparable to the effort they made, in Nazi Germany, to hide their thoughts from the Gestapo.

What Freud left, after a lifetime of code-shattering, was a world of sexual individualists. He was able to achieve this effect because his inner planets have closer connections with two of the outer planets than they do with each other or with the middle planets. The closest aspect his Mars forms is a quincunx (150 degrees) to Pluto, the symbol of sex. His Venus is conjunction Pluto, an aspect which always indicates great preoccupation with sex. For most people, the preoccupation is direct and physical. Freud was no sexual libertine personally. The intellectual orientation of the chart was too strong, and he had to make an intellectual issue of his preoccupation. The most important aspect of his Sun and Mercury is the conjunction they both form to Uranus, the Awakener.

The sextiles of Mercury to Jupiter and of Venus to Saturn, although closer in orbs, are less important in their long-range effect than the conjunctions of these two planets with Pluto and Uranus. The sextiles assured that he would be lucky in promoting his ideas, but not that those ideas would have any profound or lasting effect upon the world.

Freud worked hard to give the impression that his interest in sex was purely scientific (Mercury conjunction Uranus). His chart indicates otherwise. Sexually, he was what today would be called "uptight." By nature he was a puritan who strongly repressed any sign of hedonism in himself. He had underlying doubts of his own virility (Mars square Saturn), and like so many people with this aspect, he had to reassure himself continually by ruthlessly driving himself into the pre-eminent position in his field. Saturn square Mars often distorts the male sex drive into a drive for power to achieve supreme dominance. Since the dominance Freud sought was intellectual, the ruthlessness of his tactics was not evident to many outside his own circle. He was jealous (Mars square Saturn and four planets in Taurus) of anyone who showed talent and originality.

The same planetary configurations, plus the Sun conjunction with autocratic Uranus, show his dogmatism. Freud was a man who could not bear to be wrong about anything, or to have anyone contradict him. This is why he quarreled with Jung, Adler, Brewer, Stekel, Hirschfeld, and many more of his disciples. His animosity toward some of them who advanced doubts about his theories was so great that he refused to speak to them again.

Freud was neurotic. In spite of his dictum that everyone who practiced psychoanalysis should also be psychoanalyzed, he never discovered the repressed sexual hang-up at the root of his own neurosis. In fact, to protect himself from discovering it, he built a false image of himself that he rationalized with his own theories. This had a feedback, because once he had demonstrated to himself how well his theories worked on him, he used the demonstration as proof of their universal validity. Like most neurotics, he had a boundless capacity for kidding himself about any aspects of reality that endangered his defenses against his repressed hang-up.

Carl Jung, who once undertook to psychoanalyze Freud (at Freud's request), thought that the analysis revealed a strongly repressed incestuous attachment to a sister. Freud's resistance to any exploration of this possibility was so great that he broke off the analysis and thereafter felt such bitterness toward Jung that the two could no longer work together. In this matter, I am inclined to side with Freud rather than with Jung, for I do not find the third house of Freud's chart sufficiently afflicted to warrant a judgment of repressed incestuous desire as the root cause of his neurosis. The afflicted Saturn in the twelfth house of secrets and in the sign of siblings (Gemini) does indicate, to me, a strongly repressed jealousy (hatred) of a sibling. I believe that, in childhood, Freud felt that his father (Saturn) did not love him sufficiently but lavished too much attention upon his sister. If this judgment is correct, there might in later life be neurotic rationalizations of sibling jealousy that could be mistaken, in superficial analysis, for repressed incestuous desire. And, of course, strongly repressed hatred of a sister could help to explain Freud's lack of interest in feminine psychology.

Perhaps his whole life work was an elaborate defense against his own neurosis. Saturn, focus of the T-square, falls in his twelfth house of the subconscious mind; and it is in Gemini, the sign of the conscious mind. Wherever an afflicted Saturn falls in a chart, we have evidence of what we most fear, of what we will lie about and be mean about. Freud did not discover the subconscious mind, but he did appropriate the discovery from Charcot and Brewer, and he did build his own career on the discovery. Yet he was afraid of what he would find in his own subconscious mind. I believe whenever he came close to suspecting what was there, he retreated from the knowledge into a lie, an illusion, or a fallacy (Neptune square the twelfth-house cusp and falling in a square close to the midpoint of the Moon and Saturn).

Freud had an almost pathological admiration for his father (Jupiter culminating), but at the same time he had a strongly repressed compulsion to overcome his father, to destroy his authority (Mars opposition Jupiter). I believe this mechanism in Freud's own psyche was the source of his theory that all neurosis stemmed from the Oedipus complex.

Ambivalent emotions about the father often make a male child feel doubtful of his own virility. Freud actually feared his father (Saturn square Mars) but he repressed this fear so early in life and so vigorously that he could never admit consciously that he felt anything but the most extravagant admiration for the old man (Saturn square Jupiter). This mechanism in his psyche, I believe, is responsible for Freud's development of the theory of the castration complex.

The repressed desire to humiliate his father and the repressed fear of him made Freud feel guilty about sex, afraid to assert his own masculinity. By the curious transference of symbolism that occurs in neurotic rationalizations, he felt that somehow sexual assertion on his part was symbolic of an attack upon his father. The inner conflict was probably much stronger in Freud than it would be in most people because he was Jewish, and reverence for the father is a built-in tenet of the Jewish religion. Also, he had both Mars and Venus in aspect to Pluto, which made any sex drives he felt harder to control and more deeply rooted in the psyche than they might have been without such an anarchistic influence.

There are two solutions of such an inner conflict. The unconstructive solution is sexual impotence. The constructive one is sublimation into intellectual activity. The two solutions are not mutually prohibitive, but since Freud was married for years and had children, we had best assume that he was not impotent. Nevertheless, in the interest of safety, his sex drives were forced into abnormally shallow channels. Venus in Aries in a male chart bolsters the sense of virility by denigrating women. Although the majority of Freud's patients were women, it is astoundingly evident from all his writings that for him they were never really people. Freud could never think of women except as castrated males. He had no understanding of a female sex principle. Nowhere in his writings is there the slightest indication that gestation and child-bearing have profound sexual significance for the female, or that they are important to society. For Freud, women were simply men without penises and their psychic mechanisms were completely controlled by penis-envy. This is a typical Venus-in-Aries attitude toward women and female sexuality. It also conforms strictly to the old European code of sexual morality. Given Freud's intellectual genius, it seems odd that he did not try to shatter that aspect of the code as well as so many others. But, of course, he could not: he himself was sexually hung-up; and he was so blind to his hang-ups that he permitted serious fallacies about female psychology to become embalmed in his theories.

Contempt for women is one way to render a strong male sex drive harmless by making it shallow. Freud also used another mechanism to achieve the same end: voyeurism. The two planets that straddle Freud's Midheaven are the most undiscriminating in the solar system. Both Jupiter and Neptune are undisciplined influences for unrestrained expansion, Jupiter expands and enlarges everything it touches until it becomes overblown, like a balloon so full of air its size is awesome until you remember how vulnerable it is to a pinprick. Neptune collects everything and stows it away like a pack rat without any judgment or discrimination as to what is valuable and what isn't. Neptune fills every cranny it can dominate with trash until no one can pick his way through the accumulated junk much less examine it to see if any of it is worth keeping. Over this indiscriminately collected stuff, Neptune casts an illusion of value that inhibits anyone from examining it too closely. It is better, by far, to go on thinking the attic is full of antiques than to clean it out only to discover we're going to have to hire someone to haul it all to the dump. This is one reason Neptune has been given the rulership of the sign Pisces, which has sometimes been called the garbage can of the zodiac; and why Neptune and Pisces have been given the rulership of the unconscious mind, the garbage can of the psyche.

Both Jupiter and Neptune are planets strongly addicted to the enjoyment of vicarious experiences. Jupiter is almost as happy with the appearance of wealth as with wealth itself. It splurges through life, buying on time payments, making friends with everyone, asking only to be admired and amused. One of the things Jupiter finds most amusing is discovering something about everything that's going on, but it seldom stays long enough in one place to catch more than a glimpse or two. Jupiter is a passionate voyeur, the eternal onlooker who never really gets involved. His favorite occupations are globe-trotting and journalism. If he can combine them in one career, he's happy: then he can go everywhere, meet everyone, and sound off on everything.

Neptune is the great imitator; it borrows experience. It says the mirage must be real if you see it; the delusion must be true if you believe it, and even if the dream isn't real, it's better than reality if you enjoy it more.

These two planets straddling Freud's tenth cusp of career explain why he hit upon psychoanalysis as a method of therapy. It is psychic voyeurism for the therapist and psychic exhibitionism for the patient. It is vicarious, shallow experience for both.

The ultimate subject of all revelations is sex.

I believe that Freud abandoned hypnosis as his therapeutic method and hit upon psychoanalysis because he accidentally discovered that this sort of voyeurism was the solution to his own sexual dilemma. But it was a solution only if the patient was conscious and aware of what he was saying. With typical Neptune trickery, the long, uninhibited monologues about sex become symbolic of real sex acts. The masculine virility of the therapist is tested and proved again and again as the therapist *breaks down* the patient's resistance to the therapy. Whether male or female, the patient is always placed in a passive role, symbolized by relaxing on a couch and talking without inhibition or censorship.

Venus conjunct Pluto is the aspect symbolic of rape. Freud's therapeutic method is psychic rape. Under Neptune's beguiling deception, it was made to look respectable. With Jupiter's approval, it became fashionable. Under the bludgeoning of the Mars-Jupiter-Saturn T-square, it contributed greatly to the total demise of all codes of sexual morality. We can get used to anything if we talk about it long enough. It's easy to be a sexual individualist if you're only talking.

Freud's shattering of the ancient codes of sexual morality was an incredible achievement. The result will be with us for a long while. But psychoanalysis as a therapeutic method is already passing away; not because psychic voyeurism is not pleasurable to people who can only indulge in vicarious sex, but because, as therapy, it doesn't work. Besides, we no longer need it. We all have become voyeurs, whether we like it or not: even if we manage to escape the book, we can be sure we won't escape the movie.

Chapter VI

The Outer Planets

Uranus

The first planet beyond Saturn was sighted in 1781. For a long while it was called Herschel after the English astronomer who discovered it. Like so many of the great scientists of the eighteenth century (including Newton and Kepler), Herschel was also an astrologer. While the discovery of a new planet substantiated Newton's theories of celestial mechanics, it was most disturbing to the ancient, classical theories of astrology. Just as many scholars of the previous century had begun to scoff at astrology after Copernicus and Galileo proved that the Earth was not the center of the universe, so now the scientists went in to battle against "the ancient superstition," which could not possibly be anything other than superstition if there were planets beyond Saturn. Herschel was not among the scoffers. Keeping an open scientific mind, he reasoned that if the old planets had an effect on human affairs (as his experience indicated they did), it was logical to assume the new one would too. But what effect? Only painstaking astrological observation could answer the question.

It may be that up until 1781, the old planets accounted for everything people noticed in human affairs. But from the time of Galileo, a great deal had been happening that they preferred not to notice because it had no rational explanation and because it disrupted society in strange, unaccountable ways. The general reaction to the scientific revolution, which upset everything men had believed for centuries, was that all those new ideas were probably flash-in-the-pan heresies that would die of their own silliness if enough wicked people were killed or exiled for believing them.

Unfortunately, this gambit, so typical of Jupiter-Saturn establishments, did not work as expected. The more rigorous the persecutions, the more the new ideas proliferated. They seemed to have an uncanny fascination for ordinary middle-class people, who forgot their proper stations and spoke rudely of feudal lords and crowned heads. They began to insist they had rights no one had ever heard of before, including the right to doubt that the Earth was flat, that the laws were just, that kings were divine. They became infatuated with the notion that they had a right to worship God as they pleased. All sorts of kooks and jailbirds, alleged to be too lazy to work for a living, started printing subversive pamphlets about something they called the Rights of Man, which included unheard of things like voting, trial by jury, representation in parliaments. Weirdest of all was their insistence that they had a *right* not only to think as they pleased, believe what they pleased, but also *to govern themselves!*

It is no wonder that the forces of Jupiter and Saturn began to feel the world had come to an end. They were right. It had—at least as far as their absolute power was concerned.

All over Europe, people started behaving as if they were lords of creation, and as if nothing was impossible to human beings. When the Establishment said the Earth was flat, they sailed around it. When the Establishment said the king could do no wrong, they cut his head off. When the Establishment said that all wealth was in the land and no one should leave it because God had ordained that Adam work it forever in the sweat of his brow, they moved into the cities, invented machinery, set up factories, and in a couple of decades turned the whole economic order upside down. Then, just as the Establishment (at least in England) was beginning reluctantly to admit that the Industrial Revolution was a reality, the political revolutions began.

The first of these was the successful rebellion of the American colonies, which began at the Battle of Lexington, April 19, 1775. The new nation (still a federation of colonies) formally declared its independence on July 4, 1776, with a document that embodied the principles of the Rights of Man. Astrologers who do not argue about the correct day for the founding of this nation disagree among themselves about the correct time. Ascendants of Sagittarius, Libra, and Scorpio have all been suggested and have their adherents. The chart that works best for the majority of us, and which seems to yield the most exact predictions, is one with 8 degrees of Gemini rising. Why this time should give us the most descriptive and workable chart is mysterious, because the hour for it would have been 2:11 a.m., in Philadelphia.

The committee appointed to frame the Declaration convened on July 2, and according to John Adams, they worked far into the night. Since the Founding Fathers were a rather irascible and opinionated lot (as revolutionaries are apt to be) with many private convictions and special interests to protect, I suspect they had trouble reaching an agreement. Probably, by the early morning hours of July 4, they were exhausted with bickering and compromising and wished that whoever had had the idea of framing a declaration of independence had kept it to himself. I

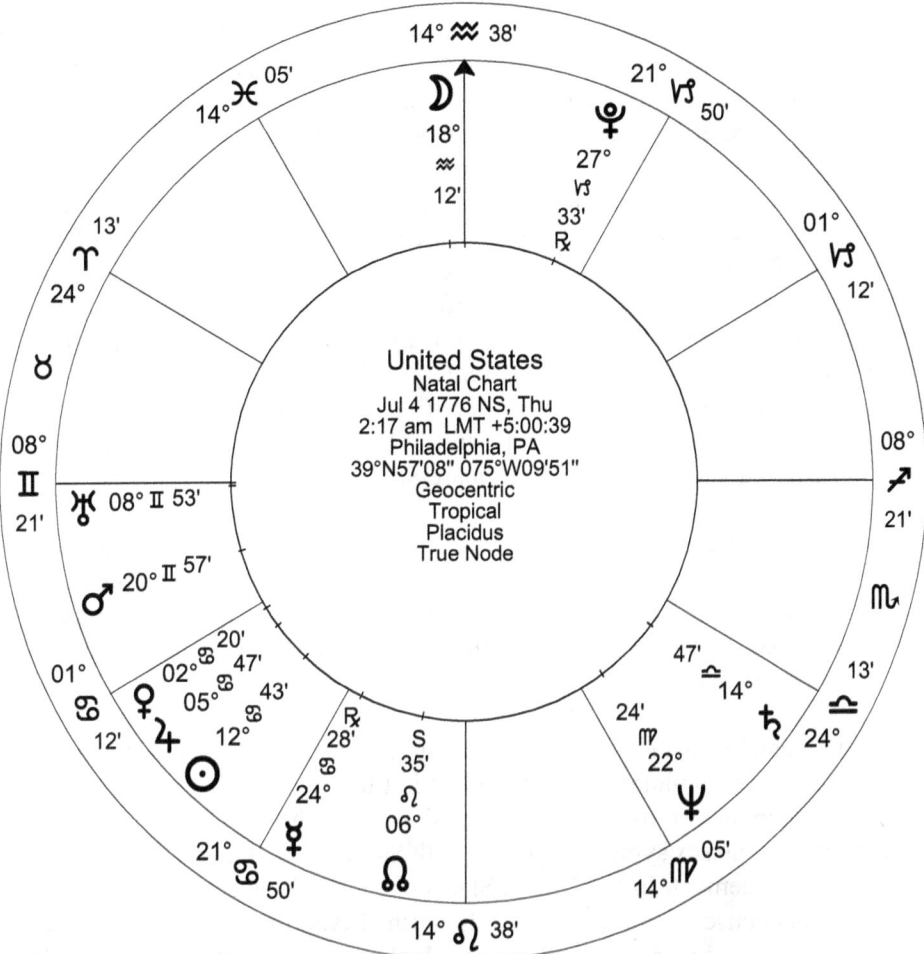

imagine that about two o'clock someone stood up, stretched, and said, "It's not perfect, but as far as I'm concerned, it'll have to do." And one last holdout said, "I still don't like that phrase 'free and equal,' Tom. I own slaves myself. And quite aside from any personal interest, I think we have enough problems without setting them free right now."

I imagine that someone reached for a pen, scratched out the word "free," and said, "Is everyone satisfied now? Then let's knock off and get ourselves a drink, if we can find a tavern still open."

Tom certainly could not have been satisfied to see his disheartening experience with the Virginia House of Burgesses repeated on a national scale. But probably he was the only one to notice the ambivalence and irony of the phrase as it was left standing: "All men are created equal."

Whatever really happened at that odd hour of the morning, it gave the new nation a horoscope with the new, still undiscovered planet Uranus exactly on the Ascendant. It has often been assumed that because so many of the framers of the Declaration were Freemasons interested in astrology, the hour was carefully selected. It may have been. Without the three outer planets, the chart is amazingly good for waging a victorious rebellion, which, after all, was the immediate concern of this revolutionary minority. Gemini, the sign of democracy and federation rises. Mars (war) is in the Ascendant trine the Moon (the people) in the tenth house of government. The Moon is trine Saturn (authority) exalted in Libra. Jupiter and Venus are in conjunction in the second house of resources, assuring that there would be enough money to continue the war. The only problem was the Sun square Saturn, indicating it would be a long, hard fight. But that aspect was also indicative of what the rebels were trying to do: upset the existing authority of the past, which they found tyrannical, and replace it with something where the people (Moon) would have power and authority in their own hands. They wanted to overthrow a king (the Sun). And if this is what you want to do, the Sun square Saturn will serve the purpose well.

All the troubles the United States has been prone to in the intervening years are effects of the three outer planets, which the founding fathers did not know existed. The revolutionary Uranus exactly rises. Mars is square Neptune in the fifth house of children, creativity, and pleasure. And Mercury, the negotiator, is in opposition to Pluto in the ninth house, which rules both the Supreme Court and foreign affairs.

We can see immediately that the effect of this revolutionary chart would tend toward revision of the ancient codes of sexual morality that prevailed in Europe. In the European chart, the Moon (women) is trapped in the twelfth house of oppression and in the twelfth sign—Pisces—of slavery. Venus, the feminine sex symbol, is square both Saturn and Jupiter, symbols of the ancient codes and their enforcement. In the United States chart, the Moon falls in the tenth house of power, in the rights-conscious sign Aquarius. It is trine Mars (the male sex principle) and trine Saturn. It disposes of the four planets in Cancer, which makes it the most powerful planet in the map. It is in its own eighth-house sign (sex and the operation of hidden power from below the surface). It has no serious afflictions from either inner or outer planets. On the contrary: it is disposed of by the powerful rising Uranus (revolution, crisis, reform), which is also without afflictions. Venus falls in the second house of money and resources, conjunct Jupiter, the code maker, and it is also without affliction.

The situation of men in the United States is much less favorable. The rising Mars (male sex principle) is square Neptune in the fifth house of love and children. Neptune is a symbol of entrapment and subversion. Afflicting Mars, it slowly, subtly vitiates and distorts the ancient principle of male dominance through sexual aggression. Mars in Gemini falls in its third-house sign, where it is much more powerful as an intellectual than as a physical force.

As a sex significator, Neptune symbolizes impotence and emasculation. It is at its absolute worst in the sign Virgo, where it has the effect of creating doubts of potency, vague fears of castration, and, if afflicting Mars, a psychological denial of the values of any frank, honest, expression of the Martian sex drives.

Because Mars is rising in the United States chart and therefore *cannot be hidden* but must find direct, visible expression, the entire country has always extolled Martian masculine values in everything *except sex*. The Martian energy is everywhere visible, but it is expressed through values that substitute for sex: violence, rebellion, lawlessness, the rape of the environment, war, heroism, pioneering on new frontiers; and, because it is in Gemini, science, engineering, and controversy over ideas. From the beginning of our history, the gun has been a sacred artifact. It is a phallic symbol. It confers the absolute power of life and death upon the impotent. The clipper ship, the locomotive, the automobile, the motorcycle, the jet plane are also phallic symbols. The latest one is the missile. Each of these, in its turn, is extolled as the marvel of the age, which will make or keep America the greatest and most powerful country in the world (an afflicted Mars rising = boasting, bluster).

Another sacred phallic symbol of Americans is often overlooked because it is an abstraction: the concept of *speed*. The idea is that the faster you go, the more powerful you are—even when you aren't going anywhere and have no reason for going there.

We have a few other sex symbols among our highly regarded artifacts that are not phallic, but uterine. These are ships in general, the covered wagon, *banks,* the darkened cinema theatre, and the space capsule. There is also a sacred uterine symbol that is an abstraction: the home. Americans always buy, sell, and live in *homes,* never houses. We seem to feel that if we repeat the word often enough, like a mantra, roots will grow under us magically and give our lives a stability that, in fact, they do not have.

The other masculine principle is the Sun, symbol of the male ego and authority. In the United States chart, it is in the third house of daily affairs, communication, and mental processes. It is in the sign Cancer, symbol of home, cherishing care, and the nourishing female breast. It is quite obvious that, for American males, the breast is a more exciting sex symbol than any other part of the female anatomy.

The third house is not a powerful position for the Sun, nor is the Sign Cancer, for here the Moon disposes of it and overshadows it with romantic, sentimental lunar values. The square of our Sun to Saturn makes it difficult for the American ego to break the bondage to ancient repressive moral codes so that it can express itself in its own unique way without strong feelings of guilt. But this square also continually presents us with problems which can only be resolved by doing just that.

The Sun is a pleasure-loving principle. One effect of an affliction to it from Saturn is to make people feel guilty if they are enjoying themselves. It exalts the value of work (Saturn) over everything else, and the harder the work, the better. Very few Americans have to work hard any more, but the less they have to work and the easier the work becomes, the more vigorously they tell themselves that they have no time for anything else. In keeping with Parkinson's Law, the papers proliferate to fill every vacant moment; and every year more American men drop dead of untimely heart attacks from the strain of pushing them around. Throughout our history, the grueling demands of the job have left little time and less inclination for the leisurely exploration of the concept that sex has great value as a means of psychic fulfillment. Sun square Saturn explains the persistence of Puritan values in American thought.

It takes a long time, perhaps several centuries, for a new civilization like ours to overthrow the moral codes and the legal and religious restraints that have been accepted without question for thousands of years. Since the great migrations to America were all from Europe, the immigrants naturally carried European codes of morality with them; and, as colonies, the early settlements were subject to European laws. After winning independence, the thirteen original states began to pass laws of their own which—again, quite naturally—reflected their own particular religious bias concerning the position of women and sexual morality. Massachusetts was a Puritan theocracy, Rhode Island was Presbyterian and Episcopalian, New York was Episcopalian and Dutch Reform; Pennsylvania, Quaker; Delaware, Huguenot; Maryland and South Carolina, Catholic; Virginia and North Carolina, Episcopalian. The anti-sex laws were most severe in Massachusetts (there, fornication is still a crime on the books), but the economic rights of women were slightly better there than in most other states.

In general, regardless of religion, the people of the new nation agreed that the only possible moral basis of society was patristic, and that women were a subspecies with the legal status of chattels who had no—or very few—property rights, and no rights at all in the disposition of their own bodies. As the original settlers pushed west and new immigrants (with the same European moral values) arrived, they carried these ideas with them across the expanding frontiers and incorporated them in the laws of each new state they founded.

A slight variation occurred in the slave states of the south, where there was a class of people even lower in status than women, and from whom (it was felt) the women had to be protected by stringent laws. In the South, even a white prostitute had to be protected from sexual assault by blacks; but this protection did not extend to black women, however respectable they were. Inevitably, people develop a cherishing attitude toward anyone they protect. The result in the South was the growth of a courtly attitude toward white women and an idealization of their position in society. (Moon in the tenth protected by the trine to Mars in the first and the trine to Saturn in the fifth.) The laws that relegated them to chattel status did not change, but custom regarding their treatment did. They were somewhat relieved of the burden of being primarily sex objects who were forced by their chattel position to gain any advantage they could through sex. The black woman became the casually treated sex object with no protection from law or society, while the white woman gradually became a person, not equal to men, but entitled to her foibles and to everyone's respect. As the symbol of white supremacy and the romantic excuse for it, she was entitled to special treatment.

The laws copied after the European codes are still on the books in most places. In spite of them, circumstances in America forced men to behave very differently toward women than they did in Europe. In the final analysis, it is the long persistence of patterns of behavior that bring changes in moral codes and sexual attitudes.

Among the early colonists and for two centuries on the expanding frontier, a woman was the scarcest of all commodities. The English colonial method gave complete property rights to the settlers, who were thus encouraged to found families and develop the land. But with typical British contempt for other races, the settlers refused to marry Indians, as the Spanish and French did readily. Therefore, in response to colonial demand, shiploads of prostitutes and petty thieves were exported straight from the Old Bailey to the New World. As the ships came in, the men would line up ten deep on the wharves, each trying to outdo the other with lavish promises of what he had to offer any lady who would take him. No one dreamed of asking questions about the past, about the lady's antecedents, or the purity of her morals. White prostitutes were rare in colonial America. Spinsters were almost non-existent. And it was far harder for a woman to maintain a state of widowhood than it was to maintain a state of virginity. This extraordinary value of women as property and status symbols in a time of scarcity is reflected in the chart by Venus conjunction Jupiter in the second house of resources, and by the Moon in the tenth of status.

In this situation the woman was not primarily a sex object. She was that prime necessity, a bearer of children. Until the end of the nineteenth century, she remained relatively scarce in many parts of the country because bearing many children under primitive conditions greatly reduced her life span. On the Eastern Seaboard, where new tides of immigrants continually poured in, she ceased to be a scarce commodity by the middle of the nineteenth century. There was a marked decline in masculine consideration for her, and an increase in spinsters, widows, and prostitutes. Still, the frontier remained open. Any woman with enough gumption could pack her bags and go there if she didn't like the way she was treated at home. Many did just that; and again, out there, no one asked questions about the past.

This reversal in behavior patterns that were thousands of years old was caused by Uranus exactly rising in the U.S. chart. Mars breaks laws individually. Uranus shatters them collectively. It does this by destroying the foundations on which they were built and presenting people with a situation so new and unexpected it is impossible to restore the old codes and make them work.

The primary, unexpected fact that faced the first settlers was a wilderness of such scope and animosity as they had never dreamed existed. Taming it, survival in it, took precedence over every ancient code of morality. They entered a Uranian new world, and from the very beginning, although they gave lip-service to the old European codes, they *behaved* in a way that continually discarded any pattern of morality that proved useless or dangerous in that new world. There was one overriding necessity: survival. What contributed to it was good, what hindered it was bad. From the beginning of the seventeenth century to the end of the nineteenth, there was always a frontier with men and women, in mortal danger of sudden annihilation (Uranus), moving west to subdue it. There was no sense taking such risks if you couldn't leave children on the land to keep it after you had conquered it. So if you were lucky enough to have a woman, you might know, in the front of your mind, that she was a chattel who had to obey your every whim; but down in your guts you knew that when she said "Hop!" you'd better hop.

As I survey the modem suburban scene, I can't see that things have changed much. But now the laws are slowly being changed to conform to the reality that has always existed.

Neptune

Neptune was discovered in 1846, when it was in the sign Pisces, to which it has such a close affinity that modern astrologers have given it the rulership of the sign. The orbit of Neptune around the Sun is about 165 years, almost twice that of Uranus (which is 84 years). This means that for many centuries these two planets, so deeply involved in social change and reform, make their all-important squares, oppositions, and conjunctions in the same signs of the zodiac. At the present (in 1971, when this book was originally published) these are the cardinal signs, which are extremely important in the United States horoscope, since we have four planets in Cancer, Saturn in Libra, and Pluto in Capricorn.

From the most ancient times, long before Uranus and Neptune were known to exist, the cardinal signs have been considered the *turning points* of the zodiac because they mark the turn of the seasons of the earthly year. Zero degrees Aries marks the Spring Equinox, the beginning of the astrological year, and by an extension of symbolism, the beginning of everything else. It is the start of a new cycle of life. Zero degrees Cancer marks the Summer Solstice, when the Sun reaches its greatest northern declination. It is the time when the seeds sowed in Aries begin to ripen and mature. Zero degrees Libra coincides with the Autumn Equinox, when the Sun crosses the equator moving south. It is the time of harvest. Zero degrees Capricorn is the Winter Solstice, when the Sun reaches its maximum southern declination. The days are short, cold, and comfortless. Men move indoors to balance the books and attend to civic and political affairs. If the harvest was bad, misery, poverty, and starvation confront them.

With the hard aspects between Uranus and Neptune made in the cardinal signs, the changeable nature of these signs is greatly emphasized. The close association between man and nature, which existed through millennia of slowly panging agrarian cultures, has been rudely violated. While both Uranus and Neptune have a good deal to do with the weather, particularly with disasters like hurricanes and floods that destroy the crops or the harvest, their most dynamic effect is in social crises which are man-created. The world no longer turns on the predictable, dependable changes of the seasons. It turns now on the unpredictable vagaries of human inventions, discontent, illusions, revolutions, and reforms.

When Uranus was discovered in 1781, it was in the sign of Cancer, moving into a square aspect with Neptune, which was in Libra. Perhaps, since Neptune had not then been discovered, the full effect of this square was not felt or appreciated. The American Revolution ended in 1781, and the process of drafting and ratifying our Constitution began as this aspect formed. While this constitution was a uniquely liberal document in its guarantees of protection of individual civil rights, it had one serious defect: it begged the question of black slavery. Uranus rules civil rights. Its sudden appearance in the consciousness of men brought an awareness of civil rights into the foreground of political concern, not only in the newly formed American nation, but in Europe as well. Neptune rules the black race, the Orient, all slaves and people in bondage regardless of race, and a class, which was largely nonexistent in 1781: the proletarian factory worker.

With the newly discovered Uranian values pressing insistently upon human awareness, it is not surprising that our Constitution went to great lengths to protect freedom of speech, religion, assembly, privacy against the arbitrary intrusion of government, while at the same time ignoring the most elemental human rights of the people ruled by the still unknown planet, Neptune. Nevertheless, all the time the Constitution was being drafted and ratified, Neptune was there in square aspect of tension and conflict to Uranus, waiting to subvert and undermine the fabric of civil rights that Uranus guaranteed.

This square between these two powerful social, political, and revolutionary planets is built into the foundation of our government. Each time the aspect recurs in the heavens, a strange social malaise afflicts our society. Conflicts of interest between the Uranian whites and the Neptunian blacks rise to the surface. Laws are passed and the Constitution is amended to repair the damage of the first oversight committed in the 1780s, laws which sincerely attempt to bring the Neptunian blacks into the fold of Uranian civil rights. Each time the repair effort is drastic, and because it has to be done on the *foundations* of the State, it endangers the structure. When the aspect passes, the country finds itself enduring a period of anarchy, corruption, and rising crime rates. No society can long endure anarchy. The response of the citizens to anarchy is always a resort to tyranny to suppress it. What was promised to Neptune under the square is taken away when the square moves on into a sextile; and this is done in the interests of preserving *Uranian* rights, which, it is generally felt, are seriously endangered by anarchy and crime.

Not quite everything Neptune promised is lost, but about ninety percent of it is. It is the nature of Neptune to promise pie in the sky, rewards without work, salvation without merit, freedom without responsibility, dreams instead of reality. He is the bagman of the heavens, regularly calling on each of us to collect our dimes and quarters, promising that surely next time we will strike it rich in the heavenly numbers game. When he's taken our last nickel, he slips us a little dope to comfort us; but he neglects to tell us, as we gratefully accept his gift, that from then on we'll have a monkey on our backs.

The problems Neptune creates are never really solved. They fade away into the background to become furtive shadows on the fringes of our consciousness. Neptune never delivers what it promises; the best it will do is give you a substitute instead, worth but a fraction of what it promised. What it does give will usually turn out to be something you can't keep, don't want, or can't use. It stays almost fourteen years in each sign, and during its tenancy, it slowly, subtly subverts the basic values of that sign. It does so under the guise of promising to give you something better, more noble and idealistic, in their place.

Since the 1780s, Neptune and Uranus have made two more squares. The first of these came immediately after the Civil War, with Uranus in Cancer and Neptune in Aries. In America, the slaves were freed, corrupt carpetbaggers invaded the South, the Reconstruction deprived white southerners of their civil rights, and the Constitution was amended to give civil rights to the blacks. In addition, crime rose to an all-time high, the Ku Klux Klan was organized, and vigilantes on the frontier and in many American cities banded together in amateur police units. Another event that resulted in the direct confrontation of blacks and whites to the disadvantage of the former was the beginning of white colonialism in Africa.

The second square occurred in the 1950s, with Uranus in Cancer and Neptune in Libra. In May, 1954, the Supreme Court handed down its famous decision in the case of Brown versus the Board of Education. This declared segregation of public schools to be unconstitutional. It was followed by legislation and other Supreme Court decisions aimed at assuring full civil rights for blacks in housing, employment, and in the courts, with severe penalties written into the laws against anyone who interfered with the efforts of blacks to exercise these rights. There were also a number of important decisions in relation to the civil rights of criminals, who are also ruled by Neptune. Once more the crime rate began to climb to another, even higher, all time high.

Another effect of the 1950s square was the beginning of American military action in the Far East, ruled by Neptune. The commitment of American troops, first in Korea and then in Indochina, resulted from our taking sides in civil wars against the native Communist factions in those countries. Neptune rules Communism. As in any conflict between Neptune and Uranus, the problems will not be solved. The promises made by both sides will not be kept, and the Neptunian people of Asia will be deluded into accepting some substitute junk at great cost to them.

In addition to these squares, there was a conjunction of Uranus and Neptune in the 1820s in the sign Capricorn. This was a reactionary political period throughout the world. Europe licked its wounds after the Napoleonic Wars. In the United States, the great surge westward across the Mississippi began. The next conjunction, also in Capricorn, occurred in the 1990s.

There was an opposition from 1905 to 1912, with Neptune in Cancer, where it is said to be exalted, and Uranus in Capricorn. This was also a reactionary political period, and, like the conjunction in the 1820s, a time of peace. But it was marked in Europe and the United States by great unrest among the proletarian factory workers and much agitation for labor unions. All over the world millions of people who were born with this configuration were killed in World War II, either as the direct result of the war or from imprisonment in the German and Russian slave camps. Many more were displaced from their homes and native countries (Cancer) and forced to immigrate to New World countries, which are ruled by Uranus.

One effect of these hard aspects between Uranus and Neptune has been an influx of rural people into urban centers. This began in the 1780s with the Industrial Revolution in England. Uranus is the significator of the Industrial Revolution. Another influx occurred in the 1820s, coincident with the potato famine in Ireland, and the agricultural reform laws in England. Many of these displaced people came to America. The Civil War gave great impetus to American industry (Uranus), so once more, when the square occurred, there was great demand for proletarian factory labor which was recruited not only in rural areas of the United States, but among the impoverished of Europe as well. The opposition from 1905 to 1912 saw a recurrence of the same phenomenon. On the last square, in the 1950s, the migration of blacks from the rural south into northern cities accelerated. There was also a heavy migration of Puerto Ricans to New York and of Cubans to Miami.

From the constant repetition of this pattern I conclude that hard aspects between Uranus and Neptune create crises (Uranus), which displace (Uranus) large numbers of people from their homes (Cancer). Urban areas promise illusory (Neptune) gains through unskilled labor (Neptune). This influx of people unable to cope (Neptune) with the stresses (Uranus) of the urban environment is the cause of the rising crime rate that follows each time such aspects are made. But the gains are illusory, the promises are not kept; instead of the lucky money, millions settle for a little junk. It is the tragedy of *Man Child in the Promised Land,* multiplied by millions.

Each time Uranus and Neptune form a hard aspect, new urban proletariats are created. (The next square from Uranus to Neptune occurs in October 2039.) Uranus rules heavy industry and industrial cities. Neptune rules the wage slaves who can barely make ends meet in their new slum environment; Neptune also rules slums and ghettos. It rules the jails that swallow up the petty criminal and the drugs he takes to comfort himself. It also rules the Communist ideology that promises him the ultimate slice of pie in the sky, and the welfare systems that are now built into economies of all countries with urban proletariats.

The repeated creation of new urban proletariats on each of the hard aspects between Neptune and Uranus has had a marked effect upon the social concepts of sexual morality, accepted modes of sexual expression, the status of women, the relation of children to their parents, and the relation of the family to society. Every time one of these hard aspects occurs, some part of the previously accepted moral code as it relates to sex goes overboard. After the repetition of five of them in less than two hundred years, we may as well admit that nothing viable is left of the codes of sexual morality that seemed so immutable when Charlemagne accepted the crown of the Holy Roman Empire.

Pluto

Pluto was discovered in 1930, when it was in the middle of the sign Cancer and near its own Node—that is, the point where it crosses the plane of the ecliptic. At the time of its discovery, it formed an unfavorable relationship with Saturn and Uranus, for Saturn was in Capricorn, making a square aspect (stress and tension) to Uranus in Aries. The first exact formation of this square was in the 13th degree of Capricorn-Aries, square and opposition the United States' Sun in the 13th degree of Cancer. The second time, the square formed in the 20th degree of Aries-Capricorn in August, 1931, when Pluto was 21 Cancer, about to make a conjunction to the U.S. Mercury and an opposition to its own position in Capricorn in our national chart. The last square between Uranus and Saturn was formed in October-November 1931, in the 18th degree of Aries-Capricorn, exactly on the node of Pluto and square and opposition, respectively, to Pluto's own degree when it was discovered.

The stressful nature of these aspects attending the arrival of Pluto on the scene of human consciousness can hardly be overemphasized. The configuration adversely affected many national charts: the foundation chart of European civilization (December 25, 800, Old Style); England (October 12, 1066, O.S.); the Chinese Republic founded in 1912 by Sun Yat Sen; the German nation (January 18, 1871); the Mohammedan civilization (July 16, 622, O.S.); Egypt (March 15, 1922), the Russian nation and civilization (Sept. 20, 862, O.S.); the French nation (July 17, 1429, O.S.). In addition to these national charts, the horoscopes of two important events are also afflicted by the Pluto-Uranus-Saturn T-square.

The first of these is the foundation chart for the history of the blacks in the United States. The record states that during the last week of August (Old Style) 1619, a badly damaged Dutch man-of-war limped into the harbor at Jamestown and unloaded a cargo of blacks. The labor shortage in Jamestown was so acute that they were immediately bid for as bond servants.

Regardless of the exact date or time of this landing, Uranus was in 26 Cancer. Whenever a heavy planet transits this degree in a hard aspect, a dynamic event affecting American blacks occurs. In the United States chart of 1776, it is afflicted by the opposition of Mercury and Pluto in Cancer-Capricorn. At the time of the Missouri Compromise (1850), it was afflicted by a conjunction of Pluto, Uranus, and Saturn in Aries. In April, 1865, when the Civil War ended, it was afflicted by Saturn in Libra. In 1954 (Brown vs. the Board of Education) Uranus in Cancer and Neptune in Libra formed a T-square over it. In April, 1968, when Martin Luther King Jr. was assassinated, Neptune formed a trine to it, and it appeared—temporarily—that the blacks gained many concessions from the riots that followed. Favorable aspects from Neptune are euphoric, but the benefits they seem to confer are illusory. By August, 1968, when Saturn in Aries squared 26 Cancer, a reactionary political trend began to appear.

In 1973 and 1974, Uranus will square this degree from the law-and-order sign Libra. Saturn will make a conjunction to it in 1975 an 1976. Pluto will begin to square it, from Libra, in 1981; Saturn will join Pluto in Libra in 1982 to augment this square. Saturn opposes the 26th degree of Cancer from Capricorn in 1990. The Neptune-Uranus conjunctions, beginning in 1993 and lasting through 1995 are in opposition to it. After these conjunctions are over, Neptune continues to oppose it through 1996. Saturn squares it from Aries in 1998 and 99, the years when Pluto itself reaches an exact opposition to the Ascendant and Uranus in the United States chart. Saturn squares it from Aries in 1998 and 1999, the years when Pluto itself reaches an exact opposition to the Ascendant and Uranus in the United States chart. Saturn will make a conjunction to the 26th degree of Cancer in late 2004, and a square from Libra in December 2011 and again in May and September 2012. Jupiter will make a conjunction to it in July 2014. Uranus will square the point in May 2017 from Aries, Jupiter will square it from Libra in 2017, and Saturn will make an opposition to it from Capricorn in 2020; and Pluto will make three oppositions to the 26th degree of Cancer from Capricorn between March 2021 and December 2022.

The orbit of Pluto is 248.4 years; therefore this will be the first time since the founding of our nation that it has crossed 7 and 8 degrees of Sagittarius. Since we have no experience or observation of the transit, it would be rash to make predictions based on it. The seventh house is designated "the enemy of the chart" and the house of warfare and strife. It is a historical fact, however, that we have fought only two minor wars with heavy planets in this position: the War of 1812, when Neptune (sea power) was there; and the Spanish-American War, when Uranus and Saturn were there. The climactic American wars, which drastically change our position as a world power were all fought when Uranus transited our Ascendant, Gemini, where it was in 1776, 1861, and for most of World War II. Other heavy planets crossing our Ascendant do not necessarily have this effect. Pluto itself reached 7 Gemini in 1889, and backed and filled over 8 Gemini until April, 1893. It was joined in this degree by Neptune in 1891 and 1892.

What happened then was the culmination of the Indian Wars, which actually began almost 275 years earlier with the Jamestown massacre. Throughout the entire period of white settlement and expansion across the continent, white men somewhere were fighting Indians. That this long-drawn-out guerrilla war finally ended when Neptune and Pluto made their series of conjunctions over our Ascendant is interesting, because these are the two planets that rule race.

Pluto rules sex as the biological principle through which nature works to create differentiation of animal species. It also rules the principle of death, which appears as soon as life forms evolve to the point where sexual contact between males and females is necessary for the propagation of the species. Pluto is thus the controlling factor in the evolutionary development of animal species and the selection of habit patterns in animals and cultural patterns in human beings that assist the species to adapt to environmental conditions and to stay alive. But it also rules the principle of devolutionary regression (death) that assures the sealing off or annihilation of any species, which through genetic defects or habit (cultural rigidity) cannot adapt to changing environmental conditions.

Neptune rules the cells and the entire chemical and hormone structure of animal organisms. Thus, if there are any actual genetic and chemical differences between races (and I understand it has not yet been scientifically established that there are), Neptune controls these differences. But remember that Neptune is deceptive in its operation. It hides the truth of whatever it rules behind a façade of illusions and deceptive appearances. So whether or not there are actual genetic and chemical differences between black, white, yellow, and red men, Neptune convinces people that there must be because they all have different colored skins and different cultures. Whether this opinion is justified or not is beside the point, because it results in war or in the suppression of one race by another.

Almost three hundred years of warfare between whites and Indians resulted from the confrontation of two alien races and two alien cultures, each considering the other to be devils. The historical evidence is that the people of the more advanced culture usually win these racial wars, even when, as in the case of the whites versus the Indians, they are initially outnumbered. If they are greatly outnumbered, however, they may win the actual war but lose the genetic battle. This happened to the Indo-European tribes (called Aryans) who invaded India in the third millennium BC. They were greatly outnumbered by the dark-skinned natives of the sub-continent. Although they set up rigid race laws to prevent intermarriage between white and colored people, the genes of the vanquished conquered in the end, for there are few white-skinned Hindus today.

We see a similar solution being tried in South Africa, where blacks outnumber whites about four to one. Neptune and Pluto are both inscrutable in their mode of action and in their purposes. They both represent cosmic mysteries we do not understand. Whether or not part of this purpose is worked out through racial confrontations and wars, I cannot venture to say. But it does seem that when people of the same race confront each other in war, the causes are rationalized as wars of conquest, freedom, economic gain, or religion. If people of two different races confront each other the actual cause of war may be the same, but before the war is over, real or manufactured racial hatred dominates the thinking of both sides. When the war ends, race laws and racial segregation perpetuate the differentiation, sowing seeds for new race wars in the distant future.

Although the reasons stated for passing racial laws are usually economic, political, or religious, taboos against racial intermarriage or copulation are soon written into the codes, with severe penalties for violation. These penalties involve loss of caste, property, and civil rights for the member of the dominating race, and—frequently—death for the member of the dominated race. A peculiarity of race laws is the vigor and cruelty with which they are enforced. It seems out of all proportion to the magnitude of the crime. In many cases, as in sixteenth century Spain, Nazi Germany, or ancient India, the penalties are more severe than for murder. The accused has almost no chance of evading them through bribery, influence, or legal manipulation, as he does against charges of murder or fraud. Race laws are usually written and enforced in such a manner that the mere accusation of a violation places the defendant in a helpless and hopeless position. In this respect they resemble laws against heresy. The result is to make everyone in the society susceptible to blackmail because the slightest appearance of transgression may result in an accusation. Just as in the case of heresy it is easy for a spiteful person to convince the authorities that where there is the appearance of smoke, there must be real fire.

All this has a drastic effect upon the moral codes and sexual customs of the society. To avoid even the appearance of transgression, the races are more and more strictly separated, which results in growing cultural divergence and inability of one race to communicate with the other, although economically, politically, and historically their lives are interwoven. Customs designed to protect the women of the dominating race become rigidified in law. These laws result in the creation of a sexually segregated class composed entirely of women, who are condemned to a harem or pseudo-harem existence, cut off—like the dominated race—from full participation in the society. A high symbolic value attaches to female virginity, which results in marrying off pubescent and pre-pubescent girls, which in turn tends to make pedophiles of the men.

Race laws and customs have many other obvious effects upon society, but they also have psychological effects that are less visible. These laws and customs have the force of taboos, which means that they exert an extreme unconscious pressure upon the individual psyche. Taboos are enforced through an unconscious mechanism of terror and guilt. The unconscious mind thinks on a different plane of reality, in a different frame of reference from the conscious mind. It cannot reason logically or express its ideas in words. Therefore, its ideas, which are emotionally grounded, enter conscious awareness in the form of symbols, myths, psychic intuitions and rituals which seem to have magical powers. All of these expressions are governed by Neptune. They are partially embodied in the culture through religion. Constant repetition of the myths, rituals, and symbols gives them external, socially sanctioned form, which both reinforces the power of the taboo and allays some of its irrational terror. This is one reason why so many people find comfort in religion. The socially sanctioned externalization of the unconscious ideas increases their magical potency, makes the irrational seem rational and unites the society on an unconscious level of being, which gives everyone who belongs to the cult an inner conviction of righteousness.

Unfortunately, the inner terror and guilt inspired by a taboo is never entirely externalized. An unresolved, unknown residue remains below the surface of rationalized action, like the invisible part of an iceberg. In periods of stress or rapid social change, such as the times we now live in, many people suddenly find the religious externalization of unconscious ideas unsatisfactory, incomplete, and comfortless. They express this by saying that the myths, rituals, and magic were merely superstitions, designed to exorcise primitive fears, which these sophisticated people no longer dread. What they forget is that the terror and guilt the original taboo inspired was never completely externalized. The once comforting religion may die of neglect, the race and sex laws may be struck from the books and old puritanical codes may be replaced with socially sanctioned licentiousness. But some residue of terror and guilt inspired by the original taboo and never resolved remains below the surface of individual and social awareness. At any time that the stress is great enough, an individual *or a society,* may suddenly begin to act out the unresolved terror to try to allay the unresolved guilt.

What an individual or society does in this acting out may take a violent form and there seems to be no control over the action. It is oddly dissociated from everyday life and may be split off from normal patterns of behavior to such a degree that people actually seem not to know what they are doing nor why. People suddenly behave as if possessed by devils; but when the outburst of violence subsides, an oddly peaceful phase ensues in which people feel cleansed as if a tremendously satisfying sexual orgasm has occurred.

This whole pattern of behavior, including the original racial-sexual taboo and the terror and guilt connected with it that was never resolved into Neptunian myths and symbols, is controlled by Pluto. The violent acting-out of the dissociated personality or society is a sexual outburst, ruled by Pluto. Repressed terror and guilt express themselves overtly as hatred. Hatred is sexually fulfilled through sadism. Whenever uncontrolled violence convulses a society, as it now convulses most of the societies of the world, long repressed terror and guilt (hatred) manifest as sadism and masochism (violence). The manifestation takes this form because the original taboo was sexual. The violence begins *after* the race laws have been revoked because it is then that the pent-up hatred of the two races for each other bursts into open confrontation. Revoking race laws must be accompanied with revocation of the sex laws that reinforced the racial taboos because, once the race laws are gone, there is no more point in the sex laws. Relaxation of racial strictures seems always to be accompanied by extreme sexual permissiveness. Sexual precociousness, sexual promiscuity, sexual liberation of women, and openly peddled pornography are commonplace and socially approved. None of this is enough to lay the ghost of the ancient taboo. Sadistic outbursts of violence are also necessary.

It is remarkable that ever since men became aware of Pluto in 1930, various races have openly confronted each other with open animosity. Simultaneously, all over the world, the ancient religions and ancient sex taboos have lost their power. Now, many societies do not merely tolerate sexual libertarianism, they approve of it and actively encourage it. What is less commonly recognized is that even those societies that still retain sexual taboos and some semblance of religion join the sexually and racially liberated ones in the rising tide of violence. But no society seems yet to recognize that this violence is another form of sexual expression; nor that sadistic violence has become the most commonplace form of sexual expression since 1930 because all societies do not merely tolerate it: they encourage it.

As soon as astrologers began to study Pluto, they recognized its connection with violence—a special type of violence that rises from the depths of society; no existing forces of law seem able to control its deadly fallout. Plutonic violence is not individualistic. It is organized group violence that functions on criminally obtained money, secret police powers, and terror. The Mafia; the bootleg mobs of the 1920s and 1930s; the Friekorps gangs and Hitler's Brown Shirts in Germany; Mussolini's Black Shirts in Italy; the Black Panthers; motorcycle gangs, like the Pagans and Hell's Angels, the Weathermen; and the juvenile street gangs that now terrorize every large American city, are all examples of the Plutonic phenomenon. They are all manifestations of a social psychopathology that has its roots in a collective doubt of masculine virility and an almost conscious awareness of individual impotence.

All these gangs arise from elements in the society that either feel themselves to be or actually are unable to cope with the social problems that confront them. In a patristic social framework, like that of every Western civilization, society's rejection of large elements, because of race, religion, illiteracy, cultural strangeness, or lack of skills the society can use, is a condemnation of the rejected group to social impotence. In a patristic society, masculinity is symbolically demonstrated by the acceptance of social responsibility, the mastery of socially accepted skills, and the assumption of authority over the society's respected institutions. Since this is the case, any large group which is declared to be, or *feels itself to be,* socially impotent is symbolically declared to be, or unconsciously feels itself to be, lacking in masculine virility.

When masses of people move from a simple, sheltered, or relatively primitive environment into a complex, indifferent, or sophisticated one, they suffer collectively from an inability to cope with the new conditions. When a nation suffers a sudden historical disaster, like the massive defeat of Germany in World War I, which destroys the entire social order, the effect is the same because no people can cope, collectively, with sudden anarchy. The logic of the unconscious mind is the logic of dreams, where one symbol or emotion is equated with another symbol or emotion which, to the rational waking mind has no relation to it. No matter what actually causes the sense of social inadequacy in a group, the unconscious equation is: social rejection equals castration.

Curiously enough, the remedy the group collectively chooses is never the attempt to overcome social rejection through the assumption of social responsibility. The solution has the same simplistic, dreamlike logic of the original equation. It runs: all the castrated must band together and prove their collective virility (power to dominate) through instituting a sadistic reign of terror. This is collective acceptance of society's rejection (symbolic castration). Group cohesion is achieved through an ideology of nihilism (conscious acceptance of social irresponsibility). Collective acts of violence bring group euphoria and psychic comfort. Group torture of selected helpless victims brings intense sexual relief, which is *proof that the tormentor is not impotent.* Sadomasochism is the only form of sexual satisfaction available to the totally impotent. It is also the only expression of sexuality in which intensity is increased through group participation.

This pattern of Plutonic sexual expression and the pattern of psychopathology that lies behind it are among the basic problems of modern society. They cannot be solved by visionary schemes to cure poverty because poverty is not the cause of the disease, but a symptom of it. All the money in the world does not make a socially responsible man of a *mafiosi* (member of the mafia) a Hitler, or a Charles Manson. The cure probably lies in massive social rejection of groupism and of all programs that encourage lumping people together into groups, then treating each individual as an anonymous entity stamped with the group seal. Human beings always have and always will form groups to cope with problems that no individual can cope with alone. The whole social process depends upon the ability to do this. But this is not the same thing as forcing people into groups, classes, or stereotypes and then denying that they are capable of performing as individuals because they wear the group brand.

The tendency to force people into groups, to classify them all by numbers, and to set up group stereotypes as absolutes by which to judge individuals, is a manifestation of Pluto. It pervades every modem society from top to bottom. Government and management by committee, the ubiquitous commissions and commission reports, team research, teams of scholars, do-good teams like Vista and the Peace Corps, mass housing, mass marketing, mass entertainment, mass therapy, mass demonstrations, and the myriad of subgroups all the way down to the hippie commune and the juvenile street gang are expressions of one side of Pluto. It is the side that segregates the amorphous mass of living protoplasm into species through a process of group differentiation that forces like to breed with like. This is the blind, underground side of Pluto, typified by the Scorpion symbol of the eighth sign of the zodiac.

But there is another side of Pluto represented by the eagle and the myth of the Phoenix rising from the ashes. The Phoenix symbolizes rebirth through the process of individuation, which can only be achieved by becoming aware of oneself as a unique entity. Pluto closely resembles the Roman god Janus, lord of the crossroads, who always looked in two directions at the same time. Pluto controls the evolution of life forms from the one-celled organism (ruled by Neptune) into many-celled species, whose differentiation he assures through sex, and whose forms he preserves through group cohesion. Then he creates mutations within each species who can only survive by capitalizing on their oddity, and by developing the courage to stand alone as unique individuals until there are enough of them to form a new group, perhaps a new species.

One of the most noticeable characteristics of the Plutonic groups in human societies is the inability of any individual member to act without group support. From the Mafia, through the committee men, on down to the street criminal, they all show a phenomenal lack of personal courage. They will all run from the scene if deserted by the rest of their group. Therefore, it seems probable that if their gangs were broken up and they could be prevented from forming new ones, most crime and violence, including corporate crime, would cease. None of these bits of protoplasm has the courage to commit a crime by himself.

The aggressive, violent planets are Mars, Uranus, and Pluto. They each have a distinctive weapon that is both a sexual symbol and a description of the type of aggressive action the planet prefers. Mars' weapons are the knife, arrow, sword, and spear. They all have to be directed by a skilled hand, and, because they can only kill one enemy at a time, the man who uses them must see his quarry from close enough quarters to a direct blow at the vulnerable spot where it can kill. Mars weapons demand a personal, one-to-one confrontation.

The Uranus weapon is the gun. It can fire anonymously from a distance and kill several unknown adversaries at once. It is most deadly in the hands of the impotent. Like the Mars weapons, however, it is a phallic symbol, exclusively expressive of male sexuality. Its distinction is that it is just as deadly in the hands of a female, which is less often true of the Mars weapons.

Pluto's weapon is the bomb, which can be secretly planted to kill unknown, unselected victims, or dropped from the air to create indiscriminate havoc. Pluto rules both the male and female sex organs. His weapon symbolizes both. The unexploded bomb is a uterine symbol; the explosion is phallic. As a symbol, it has all the sexual ambivalence of the eunuch, and all the courage of a worm.

Pluto has an extremely elliptical orbit, with great inclination to the ecliptic. Because of the great elongation of its orbit, its speed of travel through the signs is not uniform. At *aphelion* (farthest from the Sun), when it is in Aries and Taurus, it remains about thirty-five years in a sign. As it approaches *perihelion* (closest to the Sun), it rapidly picks up speed, until it is moving faster than Neptune. While in Virgo, where it remains fifteen years, it crosses the orbit of Neptune (Pluto entered Virgo in October 1956, and will leave it in October 1971). It will transit Libra for twelve years and will enter Scorpio, where it is perihelion, in December 1983. It stays only eleven years in Scorpio. After entering Sagittarius (January 1995), it gradually loses speed, but it is still travelling faster than Neptune when the twenty-first century begins.

During all this time, Neptune continues to plod along at its steady, invariable rate of fourteen years to a Sign. When Neptune entered Libra in 1942, it was in a sextile aspect (60 degrees) to Pluto in Leo. Because Pluto has been picking up speed since then, this aspect has frequently become exact and will continue to do so until the end of the century. This long drawn out sextile relationship between the two outermost planets is the key to understanding the twentieth century and the sexual revolution that is so much a part of its changing values.

Of course this aspect has occurred before in human history, but only as an effect between two unknown planets. Every 244 years Pluto reaches its perihelion and crosses inside the orbit of Neptune. But Neptune, whose orbit is 164.8 years, is not always in a sextile relationship to it at the same time. The last time the aspect occurred with these planets in the same orbital positions (that is, Leo-Libra to Sagittarius-Aquarius) was at the height of the Renaissance, from roughly 1460 to 1530. Like the present, that was a period of rapid change, the disintegration of old values, unremitting war, terrible violence, new discoveries, uncontrollable crime in the streets, and an anything-goes attitude toward sex. It was also a period of unprecedented prosperity and inflation.

Here we are concerned only with the extreme sexual permissiveness of the aspect, although it is undeniable that the total breakdown of social institutions and values has an effect upon sexual attitudes. Indeed, it is the sense of *unreliability* of social institutions in a rapidly changing world that creates the feeling of helplessness and fear of the loss of individuality associated with alienation, as we now call it. Alienation is the feeling that we are abandoned by society in a world without values. It is a "nobody-loves-me" feeling; the reaction to it is: so why should I love anyone? People who feel loving and beloved do not go in for sexual aberrations, licentiousness, or perversions. These are attempts to get kicks out of love by people who cannot love.

The sextile aspect is permissive, opportunistic, and lucky. It is lazy and optimistic. It has a God-will-provide attitude, so why should I kill myself working? It expects to be taken care of, and, as we can see from the generation born with it since 1940, it usually is. When it occurs between tricky Neptune, which prefers illusions to reality, and criminally inclined, violent Pluto, those who think they are not properly taken care of feel that they have a *right* to steal, mug, and murder to get what they should have been given in the first place.

Neptune rules impotence. Pluto rules sex in the generalized biological sense. Under the influence of the permissive, anything-goes sextile, the sexually disadvantaged (impotent) feel they have a right to steal any fun they can by whatever peculiar or violent means. Like the street criminal under the influence of the same aspect, they feel they're only taking what should have been given to them in the first place. Under this influence, aberrations that are normally kept hidden are, instead, pushed into the open. Homosexuality is one of them. During the Renaissance it achieved the same sort of public prominence and tolerance among the upper classes that it has today. The rise of a new Puritanism, which seems always to occur in reaction to the permissiveness of this sextile as soon as the aspect fades, will no doubt put the *quietus* (death or release) to it again.

Chapter VII

Uranus as a Sex Significator

Homosexuality-Rebellion

Until the discovery of Uranus, and for about a century thereafter, astrologers laid the blame for homosexuality on Mercury. Their reasoning was simple and logical: Mercury was the androgynous, sexually immature, and sexually-neutral planet. They made little progress in understanding the problem, however, because Mercury is almost impossible to use as a sex indicator. It is by nature indifferent to sex, and regardless of sign or aspect, planets never behave in a manner contrary to their basic natures. The only times Mercury becomes a sex indicator is when the individual never outgrows the masturbatory orientation of childhood (ruled by Mercury); or when his indifference to sex and his lack of understanding of its emotional values cause him to be thoughtlessly cruel to those who love him.

Mercury's indifference to sex makes it emotionally shallow. The physical and emotional suffering it may inflict upon others through thoughtless infidelity, verbal mockery, and half-hearted, emotionally uninvolved love-making show in the charts of the people who feel the suffering, not in the strongly mercurial chart of the person who carelessly inflicts the suffering. Nothing a person is incapable of experiencing manifests in his chart. Therefore, if the strongly Gemini or otherwise mercurial person claims that he is suffering from unrequited love, his distress correlates with other planets. Or he is exaggerating to dramatize himself, as Mercury will sometimes do.

Modern astrologers have a rapidly increasing number of clientele who are homosexual. While trying to help them, we soon notice that the homosexual temperament is not indifferent to sex. On the contrary, the homosexual is constantly and passionately involved with sex and with the social and economic problems that arise at every turn of his life because of his aberration. Nothing is simple for homosexuals. Not for one moment does society allow them to forget that it cannot tolerate them or their habits. If she tries to hide his aberration, she is in danger of blackmail. If she admits it frankly, she is in danger of being sent to jail. The industrial, bureaucratic societies of the Western world decided early in the nineteenth century that the homosexual image was bad for business. Therefore, most homosexuals who succeed in finding employment with the government or large corporations are not promoted into management or executive positions, as are people with lesser qualifications who are considered "more reliable." Since homosexuals, as a group, exhibit a normal cross section of intelligence, being forced to work at dreary, monotonous jobs with no future is a source of further frustration.

At any time, homosexuals may be sexually, intellectually, professionally, economically, or socially frustrated. They are seldom allowed to forget that they are outcasts, that every relationship they form is precarious, and that if they trust any person or situation they are liable to be hurt. Since the homosexual person is aware that all these problems arise because of their sexual orientation and society's disapproval of it, how can they be indifferent to sex? And how can they fail to be deeply involved with it emotionally?

The fact is that society, other people, and everyday life all function badly for the homosexual. How society functions for any individual can be discovered by the condition of the Moon in the natal chart.

I selected ten charts from my files in which homosexuality posed a severe psychological problem for the individual. They are all cases where the client consulted me repeatedly, so that I became thoroughly familiar with how the life malfunctioned, not only in relation to sex, but also in relation to employment, to other members of the family, and to the whole range of emotional affect in the individual's dealings with society.

In eight of the ten charts, the Moon was severely afflicted by Uranus. In four, it was also afflicted by Saturn, in one by Mars, and in one by Pluto. There were two cases that lacked afflictions of the Moon from Uranus. In one, Uranus afflicted the Ascendant, Mercury, and Venus, but the Moon was without any afflictions at all and had some good aspects. This person actively fought tendencies to homosexuality, with the result that he became indifferent to any sort of sex, although he is not impotent. His general adjustment to society has been good. It functions well for him. He has no chip on his shoulder about other people's treatment of him. His reaction toward checks and hindrances from the outside world is mature. He does suffer from emotional shallowness or reticence, which he overcomes by an active kindness toward others.

In the other case where the Moon escapes affliction from Uranus it is in a grand cross with Saturn, Neptune, and the Sun. This person is a paranoid schizophrenic who so far has evaded hospitals, although he has not always managed to stay out of jail. He is blatantly, even proudly, homosexual; but he has so little insight into the magnitude of his problems that it is impossible to say what, if anything, about his wholly malfunctioning life really bothers him. His emotional reaction to the world and to others is that of a small child, perhaps four or five years old. Although he has superficial artistic talent and a kooky sort of intelligence, he is quite unable to earn a living. Like a child, he manages to place himself in situations of dependency upon others, who are thus forced to take care of him. His manner is light-hearted and cheerful. He feels no responsibility for himself, for others, or for anything he does, because he believes he has been selected to govern the world in some future time, when it will be taken over by powerful extraterrestrial forces. He is in touch with these forces, which already acknowledge him as the king of the world. Everything he does is therefore kingly, and cannot be wrong.

He is included in this list in spite of his schizophrenia because his personality and temperament exemplify the classic picture of the homosexual type. But in everything he does, he plays a role with his eye on the audience to judge its effect upon them. It may be that he is also playing his homosexual role, and this could account for the absence of Uranian afflictions to his Moon and for the fact that his homosexuality does not trouble him. An interesting feature of his chart is that every planet is afflicted except Mercury and Uranus, the two usually associated with homosexuality. They are in trine to each other, but otherwise unrelated to anything else in the chart.

In my example charts, Mercury is almost always favorably aspected. In one case it is opposition Uranus, and in another it is square the Moon. Both of these people have had difficulty obtaining higher education, for their attitude toward conventional schooling is rebellious. The commonest Mercury aspect is the conjunction to Venus, but it is also found trine the Moon, sextile Neptune, conjunction Mars, trine Jupiter, and trine Saturn. Other astrological studies of homosexuality seem to confirm that Mercury is usually strong and well aspected. In spite of the emotional difficulties of their lives and the many stresses related to a malfunctioning Moon, the intelligence is sharp and inventive. Mercury is the problem-solving planet. By nature, it seeks the way out of every sort of trap. Therefore, in the typical homosexual life, it gets plenty of exercise because the casual human relationships that most people take for granted can create traps and problems for the homosexual. In his struggle to protect himself from society and to function in it, he is required from an early age to make rational (Mercury) assessments of his difficulties and to take clever (Mercury) measures to circumvent them. The better the Mercury is in the homosexual chart, the sooner he will recognize his outcast (Uranus) position and try to invent (Mercury) a way of life that assures him a good deal of personal privacy, and where talent and ingenuity may force society to yield him a living in spite of his nonconformity to its standards.

In Western society, since the discovery of Uranus, and probably for several generations before, this rational (Mercury) solution of the homosexual's problem has always cost him dearly. The price is distortion of emotional affect (Moon). If we are correct in assuming that one astrological clue to homosexuality is an affliction from the unstable Uranus to the emotional Moon, it seems probable that acute emotional pain suffered in childhood (the Moon) in some social situation (Uranus) is at the root of the homosexual personality.

The child's earliest and most important social situation is the family. Although Freud knew no astrology, he must have recognized this Moon-Uranus effect in his homosexual patients because he said that an unresolved Oedipus complex *always* lay at the bottom of homosexuality. Unfortunately, it also seemed to lie at the bottom of every other aberration in Freudian psychology. As astrologers, such theoretical vagueness can never be good enough for us. We have to know why the person who is homosexual responds to emotional pain suffered in childhood by a very specific distortion of emotional affect, which becomes more pronounced with age.

This does not mean that the male homosexual necessarily adopts feminine mannerisms or tries to play a feminine role. It is a refusal to respond emotionally (the Moon) to stimuli that normally excite the male psyche and bring it emotional release from tension. It is as if the homosexual personality insulates itself against such stimulation, and by refusing to feel any response, protects itself against a recurrence of the childhood pain. The result is emotional poverty, which leads to the displacement of emotional values onto things or situations that distort them still further. Fetishism is an example of such displacement of emotional values. Temper tantrums over trivial incidents that have no personal meaning are another—like an exhibition of extreme anger at the grocery store because it was out of black pepper, or exaggerated sulkiness because it rained and ruined plans to go swimming. Another example is the persistent referral of everything that happens to make someone the target of the world's animosity. This attitude says, "The pipe burst deliberately to inconvenience me," or, "They went on strike just so I couldn't get my new car."

Of course these are childlike reactions, and we all recognize them as signs of emotional immaturity when we see them in adults. But in the homosexual, exaggerated emotional response to trivial causes or to stimuli apparently unrelated to the emotion displayed are so noticeable that they are exploited by writers and actors to mock them. It is little wonder that the homosexual, stereotyped and lampooned in this way, feels isolated and angry. Since unreleased emotional tension becomes unbearable, it must find outlets in inappropriate ways. But emotional tension released in inappropriate ways does not bring relief. Instead, it brings increased inner stress, discontent, and isolation from society.

What emotional outlets does the homosexual give up when he retreats from masculinity? To find out, we must look at the qualities and nature of Mars, symbol of the male. Mars is aggressive, violent, physically active, energetic, warlike, quick to anger, outspoken, tactless, danger-seeking, woman-chasing, direct, rash, insubordinate, honest, and scornful of the devious and the shrewd. An emotional stimulus to Mars is always perceived as a *challenge* to which he reacts instantly with a response as physical and direct as the situation permits. The response is active, unpremeditated, and visceral. Mars rules the adrenal glands. Stimulus to a Martian quality results in an upsurge of adrenalin into the system. The amount of adrenalin released is in proportion to the power and urgency of the stimulation that is felt as an emotional pressure demanding immediate outlet. This release is achieved, however, only when the action taken is a suitable response to the stimulus and is directed toward an appropriate object. The choice between what is appropriate and what is not is instantaneous and conditioned by the kind and power of the emotion demanding release.

The process is one of instant judgment, in which life and death decisions are made in a split second for what appear to be instinctive reasons, biologically determined. It is a built-in system of problem solving on the emotional level. The survival of every animal species, including humans, and of every human society depends upon it. It is the mechanism that comes to our rescue when to reason is useless, when there is no time to think. It drives us from a burning house, directs the split-second action that prevents an accident, pushes us into the water to save a drowning child, makes us fight to defend our lives or run from a danger too powerful to overcome.

When the emotional power of the Martian response finds appropriate goals for its release, the result is life persevering, and a sense of victory floods through the individual as emotional tension subsides. When directed toward inappropriate goals, the result is life defeating and may even be fatal. Only a fool stops to argue with a tiger.

A retreat from masculinity is a rejection of this whole complex of Martian values. It is a deflection of the Martian emotional challenge and response to inappropriate goals. There is no sense of triumph when the emotional tension is released. Instead, there is a sense of strong dissatisfaction, of worthlessness. The individual feels beset by unresolved problems and inadequate to cope with a dangerous world. As the inner stress of unreleased tension builds up, the emotions inspired by a sense of danger begin, vaguely, to pervade all relationships, and emotions are repressed in an attempt to feel nothing.

When people reach this stage, they begin to seek protectors and protective situations—for example, the feminine personality, which is the emotional syndrome of Venus. The effort is self-defeating because it is biologically inappropriate. The result is a caricature. But the purpose behind it is to gain the protection from a dangerous world that most societies have decreed is proper to give to women, children, and slaves.

Uranus is the planet that symbolizes the exploration of new frontiers and the expansion of the society into new territory. We happen to live during a moment of history when wars of expansion are regarded with horror. We associate them with paranoid fear for national security (Saturn), and with a greedy desire for imperial power (Jupiter). But through the thousands of years of human history, there have been countless times when migration into new territory became essential for the preservation of the people. When changing weather conditions destroy the nomads' grazing lands, they must move or die. When changing economic conditions or over-population condemns millions to slow starvation, they must emigrate in vast numbers or die. Extreme political tyranny may have the same effect.

In terms of numbers, the greatest migration in recorded history consisted of the wave after wave of Europeans who moved to North America from 1700 to 1920. And who, immediately on their arrival, started pushing across the continent to the Pacific, fighting Native Americans and the wilderness at every step. Just so, the ancient Phoenicians carried their civilization from Tyre to the British Isles, the Romans pushed theirs to the Rhine and the Danube, the Chinese established trading outposts beyond the Gobi desert, the Byzantines colonized the Balkans and southern Russia, and the modern Jews founded a viable state in Israel.

All this activity is a function of Mars. It occurs in response to a strong emotional compulsion which each individual feels personally as an inner drive applying only to himself. The fact that millions of others are responding to the same inner urge hardly concerns him. In the same way, several million men throughout the world are undoubtedly falling in love at the same moment in response to the Mars urge to procreate; but for each individual man the experience is unique, intensely personal, visceral, and of dramatic importance. It is always so when we respond to the goading of an inner planet, for they govern that part of our lives and our psyches where we believe we have freewill.

In the retreat from masculinity, however, the homosexual person is responding emotionally to Uranus, and sometimes to Neptune. These are planets of strong social compulsion that make us feel that we are not really individuals, but fragments of some large, immensely powerful organization (Uranus) or collective (Neptune). We do not feel that we have any real control over these organizations or collectives. We do not believe that any action or decision of ours can impress them or change them. Under the goad of Mars, one man sets out to explore the world, feeling that he alone made this dangerous decision, and that only he will be responsible for what happens to him. Under the goad of Uranus, he leaves because he is hired to do so. Larger interests, for corporate or national reasons, support or subsidize his venture. Columbus, subsidized by Ferdinand and Isabella; the adventurers who went to Virginia and India, financed by English joint stock companies; and the American exploration of the Moon are examples of Uranian pioneering. Mars symbolizes the lonely hero of the Daniel Boone type. Uranus symbolizes the group of pioneers or adventurers of the Conquistador type who act in response to a social need with the support of powerful elements in the society.

It is characteristic of the homosexual to feel that his condition is not his fault. Something happened to him or was done to him that caused it. His mother was a bitch, his father was a bastard, he grew up in the slums, he was a poor little rich boy, someone raped him when he was ten, or any of countless other quite common experiences is to blame. He feels that he is a misfit in society, an unloved outcast, a freak. These are Uranian emotions, responses to the helplessness we all feel when suddenly confronted with Uranian social pressures or Uranian disasters. All the inner planets symbolize some facet of individuality that we take for granted. In our everyday affairs, which are governed by inner planet impulses, we assume that society will leave us alone to make our own free choices. The homosexual, however, does not feel free in these matters, but somehow pressured, and believes that society prevents the freedom to make choices.

Actually, there is no chart that does not suffer from some restraint upon one or more of the inner planets, inhibiting the freedom of the will. But usually we recognize such situations as problems central to our lives—as personal problems. They may not be wholly of our own making, but we feel that they are within our power to solve, that through *individual* choice we can cope with them. Stressful aspects between the inner planets do not lessen our sense of individuality, but may actually increase it by urging us to find unusual solutions.

The effect of pressure from an outer planet is quite different. It confronts us with problems that we feel are not personal, not unique, but general to the society. It stifles us with the sense that masses of people are pressing in upon us, or that we are in the grip of world-shaking, uncontrollable events. It gives us numbers Instead of names. It converts our most heartbreaking experiences into statistics on a graph. It pushes us into groups and classes, where we begin to feel like faceless automata, like things to be manipulated, like non-people.

The three outer planets behave like tyrants dictating the pattern of our lives. The reaction of the individual who feels heavy stress from one of them upon an inner planet is typical of our reaction to human tyranny: rebellion (Uranus); sabotage (Neptune); undifferentiated, impersonal crime (Pluto). The challenge of the outer planet is felt as a privation of the freedom to be an individual, a privation of choice. Unfortunately, although the outer planets act primarily upon the individual through social changes and cataclysms, the arena where the individual acts out his rebellion is usually the private field of his own psyche. Society dares us to prove that we are individuals, but also lets us know that no individual act of ours will make the slightest impression upon it. So the rebellion moves inward, forcing us to prove our individuality to ourselves.

The rebel-without-a-cause syndrome is a typical reaction to Uranian pressure. It is a stubborn, undifferentiated resistance to conformity or to any routine that can be construed as conformist. On its constructive side, Uranus idealizes human cooperation, so the rebel-without-a-cause refuses to cooperate. These people make careers of upsetting apple-carts—their own and other people's—to get even with everyone by impressing them with their own naughtiness. They assume that the person or people who are symbolized by the inner planet that Uranus afflicts in their own charts love them, but once did some unspecified wrong that cut off their individuality. Any efforts to appease rebels, and especially efforts to make them happy, result in intensified naughtiness, until finally the rebel's own personality becomes as diffuse, rootless, and lacking in direction as their causeless rebellions.

Where Neptune afflicts an inner planet, particularly the Sun, Moon, or Venus, and Pisces or Virgo is strongly emphasized, there is sometimes a will to annihilation of the self. Such clients are difficult to help because they have an unlimited capacity for deceiving themselves. The astrologer or psychiatrist may recognize the deceptions, but there is little he can do because, as soon as the client becomes aware of one deception, he flees into another. Neptune is the planet of the copout; the roles it adopts serve a protective purpose.

To answer this we must realize that it is only since the discovery of the outer planets that men have become consciously preoccupied with sex as a *psychological* factor of importance in the formation of their characters and destinies. This psychological preoccupation with sex has occurred only in the Western World. It is a phenomenon of European culture, felt only where that culture has dominated thought. Under the influence of this psychological probing, many sexual acts and expressions have been labeled aberrant or perverted, which, in other countries and in other ages have been considered nothing to make a fuss about. Unless there is social scorn or criticism attached to an act, people who perform that act do not feel psychological stress as a result. They may even be praised and admired for their unusual aptitudes.

In his journals, Tschaikovsky often mentions the pain his homosexuality caused him, and his fear that anyone would discover it. His was probably a typical attitude. Under such strong pressure from society not to betray any aberration, most men who felt a slight inclination toward homosexuality undoubtedly suppressed it, married, and raised families. Others probably remained celibate and led sexless lives or went into the Church, taking vows of celibacy.

But in many times, cultures, and religions, homosexuality is not unlawful. It is neither encouraged nor discouraged. In most societies, marriage has always been a legal contract entered into for the financial good of the respective families. Women were chattels with no legal recourse against any aberration their husbands might practice. What the men did, both in and outside their harems, was their own business. In such societies, a man would hardly feel psychological stress from a sense of sexual inadequacy: he could always beat his wife to death if all else failed, and no one could criticize or condemn him for it. In other words, sex in such societies is an inner planet matter, subject to what the individual male believes is his own free choice.

During the great age of Greece, in the fifth and fourth centuries before the common era, homosexuality was considered the highest form of love. Plato, the most brilliant homosexual of all time, honored it with his name, and the scholars of his Academy assiduously cultivated it. In another time and place, most of them probably would have been quite normal. Even then, they made love to women when it suited their convenience—as Alcibiades complained he had to do for so long to keep the queen of Sparta happy.

Homosexual slaves and prostitutes have always been in great demand in Moslem countries. The Mamelukes, who attained great power in medieval Egypt, were originally imported from Europe to serve homosexual purposes. Although scorn was attached to them because they were slaves, they suffered no stress or adversity because they were homosexual.

As an exclusively inner-planet phenomenon, homosexuality is associated with aspects—usually stressful between the Moon and Mars, and between the Moon and Saturn. I have a few such cases in my files, where there are no added afflictions to the Moon from an outer planet. These people are aware of the problem, can clearly state the incident or event that led to their homosexuality, and want to be cured. They do not feel that circumstances beyond their control forced them into a situation where they had to become homosexuals to prove that they were individuals.

Somerset Maugham and Gertrude Stein

W. Somerset Maugham and Gertrude Stein were both self-acknowledged homosexuals. Their lives and careers show many other similarities. They were both well-known writers; both spent most of their lives in foreign lands; both had a strong affiliation with Paris, were greatly influenced by French culture and by the Impressionist and Post-impressionist movements in art; both suffered greatly from the German invasion of France in the Second World War; both formed great collections of modern paintings accumulated at bargain prices when their friends, the painters, were unknown or unpopular; both studied medicine and abandoned it for literature; both died in France. They were born nine days apart.

There is no known birth time for either Maugham or Stein; therefore, the charts presented here are of the Johndro type and cast for the place of birth. If Miss Stein's map were moved to Paris, where she lived most of her life and did most of her work, the house cusps would be nearly the same as for Mr. Maugham's. This is because the Johndro chart gives primary consideration to the place of birth or residence, rather than to the time of birth as in the conventional horoscope. The theory behind the Johndro system is that there is a close interplay between the individual and the environment. Johndro himself was quite fatalistic in his reading of these charts. He felt that the particular cosmic influences at work in the place where an individual happened to be had a physical, materialistic effect upon him, which was so fateful that no exertion of freewill or psychological development could change the outcome. The individual could exert his freewill to change his fate only by deciding not to go to a place where he would be adversely affected, or by moving away from it as quickly as possible. A Johndro chart can be cast for any person or event if the place and date are known, but not the time. In this it differs from the usual solar

74/Sex and the Outer Planets

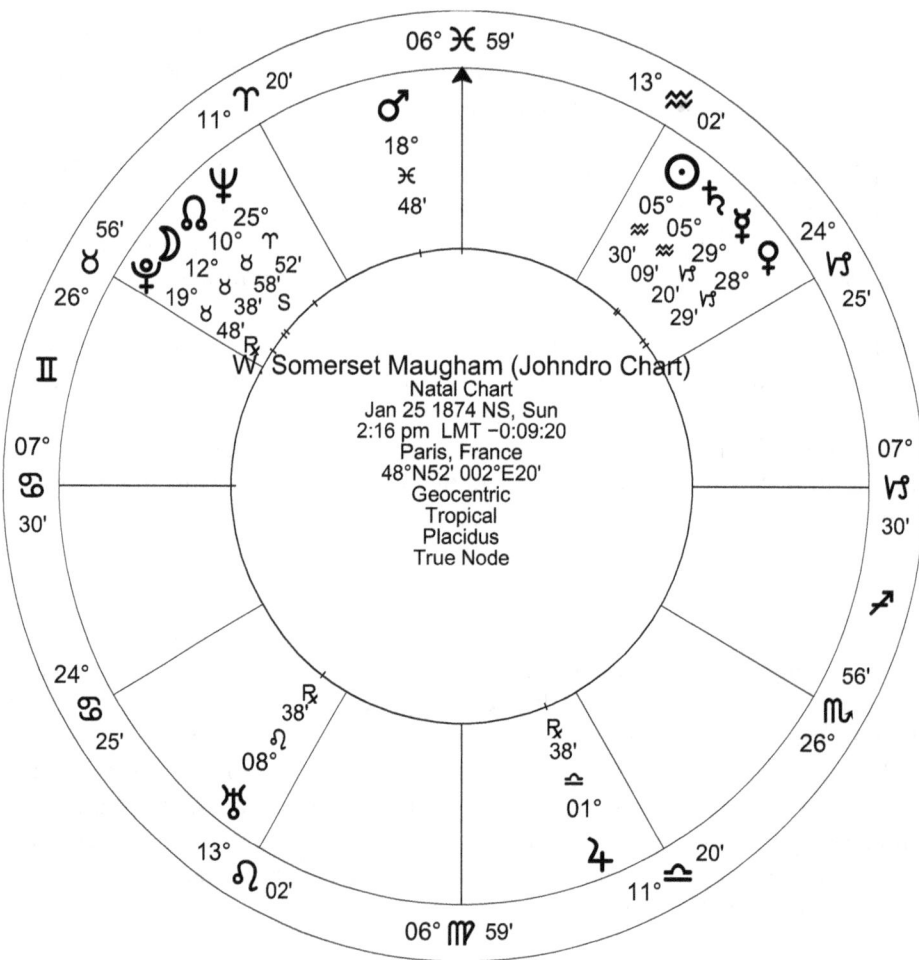

chart, which is often cast for people and events when both the hour and place of birth are unknown. (The formula for casting Johndro charts is given in Appendix A.)

Stein and Maugham were homosexuals regardless of where they lived. They carried this psychological conditioning with them wherever they went as part of their temperaments and characters. No doubt other people in different environments reacted differently, so that they found some environments more permissive and congenial than others. Stein found France more permissive than America, and Maugham preferred it to England. It should be noted that Maugham was less willing to come to terms with his homosexuality than was Miss Stein. He once wrote that until he was about thirty he believed he was normal most of the time and queer only occasionally; he reached middle age before he could admit that he was queer most of the time, and normal very rarely. There is no record that Miss Stein ever thought herself normal, even rarely.

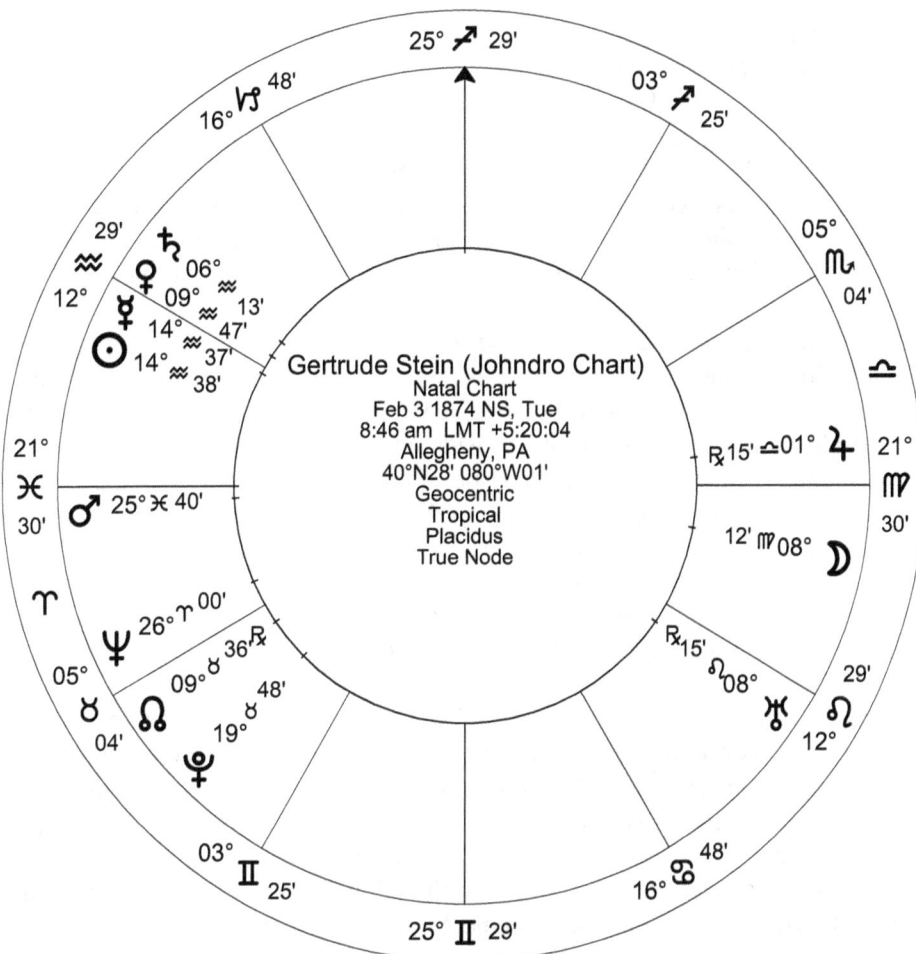

Notice the close square of the Moon to Uranus in Maugham's chart, with the Sun-Saturn conjunction, from the eighth house of sex, in opposition to Uranus. The Venus-Mercury conjunction, also in the eighth, is square Neptune. I conclude from this that there was a strong element of masochism in his temperament, but that he was able to resolve this constructively through his work because Venus and Mercury were in trine aspect to his Jupiter, ruler of his sixth house of work.

The square between Mercury and Neptune probably explains the fact that Maugham stuttered badly. In his great autobiographical novel, *Of Human Bondage,* he gives his hero a club foot in place of the speech defect. This is an interesting bit of psychological symbolism because the club foot was the distinguishing mark of Oedipus, whose name means "swollen foot." The selection of this symbol was probably unconscious and not influenced by Freudian theory:

Maugham wrote his novel during the years 1912 to 1914, before Freudian ideas were widely known outside psychoanalytical circles.

In Miss Stein's chart, Venus has moved on to form a conjunction to Saturn and both are in opposition to Uranus. The Moon in Virgo forms a quincunx to both Venus and Saturn, but is otherwise unafflicted. Mercury has moved on to form an exact conjunction with the Sun, and they too are opposing Uranus, although with rather wide orbs for a separating aspect. The Sun and Mercury have also moved into orbs of square to Pluto, ruler of the eighth house of sex.

Miss Stein's chart is interesting also because it has the rebel aspect, Mars opposing Jupiter, across the Johndro first and seventh houses of personality and relations with the public. Her personality was somewhat irascible, and she often seemed to go out of her way to offend the conventional morality and ideas of people she considered dull or stupid. She was less successful in gaining acceptance of her work (a characteristic of this aspect) than was Maugham. Both as a writer and a person, she was more controversial than Maugham. She also developed the guru status so noticeable in the late years of people born with Mars opposition Jupiter. She gathered young disciples around her from literary and artistic circles. The influence of her ideas upon them may actually be more important than her own work. Many of them, like Ernest Hemingway, gained a popularity she herself never achieved.

Jupiter intercepted in her seventh house of war and public enemies, in trine aspect to Saturn, ruler of her eleventh house of friends, probably saved her life during World War II. Although she was born Jewish and American, she refused to leave France. She continued to live in a small house in the country outside Paris, and although the peasants and townspeople all knew who she was and any of them might have gained favor with the Nazis by turning her over to them, they all protected her and saw to it she was fed, even though it meant sacrificing some of their own slim rations. She was also very popular with the American soldiers who sought her out after the war: they found both her outspoken, unconventional ideas and Alice B. Toklas's superb cooking stimulating.

It must not be assumed because these two charts are presented here as examples of male and female homosexuality that all people born about the same time were homosexuals. Such a conclusion would be as erroneous as it would be to say that, because Gertrude Stein and Somerset Maugham were both writers, everyone else born about the same time was also a writer.

Chapter VIII

Neptune as a Sex Significator

Masochism

Neptune's influence is the most difficult of all to evaluate. It is so subtle and operates in such devious, hidden ways that even after the influence is long past it may be impossible to judge the full extent of its insidious damage. All the outer planets create irrevocable social change. Uranus does so openly, through political revolution, dramatic scientific discoveries, and self-conscious social reforms adopted to further a utopian ideology. Pluto does so through devastating wars, tyrannical dictatorships, and slow but massive changes in the economic structure that results in the redistribution of wealth and a shift of power from one social class to another.

Except in the material matters ruled by Neptune, such as naval power, oil, chemistry, photography, and the fine arts of painting and ballet, Neptune operates below the level of consciousness. It is the ruler of the unconscious mind, both in individuals and in the collective. It is the influence that works while we sleep, insidiously changing our values and personalities in hidden and mysterious ways. Brutal oppression and social injustices may exist for centuries, crying out for Uranian reforms, but nothing happens. Starvation, serfdom, slavery, tyranny—every imaginable human misery—may be accepted without complaint, condoned, even exalted by the people who suffer most, as a system ordained in heaven that nothing can change. Until suddenly, for no visible reason, masses of people begin to dream romantic, impossible, glamorous dreams. They begin to imagine what life would be like if these dreams should come true. They begin—whole masses of them at once—to feel a strong inner compulsion to cop out of the oppressive status quo, to resist it passively, to flee from the daily grind of a reality that yields them nothing into a blissful dream world that assures them of future salvation. Once a mass of people, collectively, feels this degree of longing for a dream to come true, they move into the next phase of Neptunian influence: faith that it *must* come true.

Then, out of the mass of believers in the dream, a spokesman emerges who puts their longing into words, who plucks the dream from the hidden recesses of the collective unconscious and makes it stand out objectively. He projects their secret longing out upon the external world. They listen to him and follow him because he speaks with the voice of authority, saying what *they have always known in their hearts was the truth.* For the early Christians, Paul was the spokesman of the dream; for the Germanic Protestants, it was Martin Luther; for the pre-revolutionary French, it was Jean-Jacques Rousseau; for the American Blacks, it was Martin Luther King; for twentieth century Hindus, it was Gandhi.

In social, political, and sexual matters, Neptune acts through and upon the unconscious, and does so with compulsive power. Neptune is the lord of the *illusion of reality*. He can operate only upon a non-materialistic plane of thought, dreams, emotion, spirit, illusion, hypnosis, faith. He is the magician who distracts our attention with smooth talk so that we will believe he really pulled the live rabbit from the empty hat. The moment we become conscious of the trick, it becomes meaningless. The childlike awe we felt at witnessing the miraculous materialization of living rabbit is transformed into the rational curiosity of Mercury that demands to know how it was done. Neptune is the planet whose right hand never knows what the left hand is doing. He is the master of the shell game, and his power over us lasts exactly as long as we believe there is really a pea under one of the shells.

The cry of Uranus is: "Sleepers awake! The revolution is at hand!" But Neptune whispers, "Sleep on! The miracle will happen while you dream!" Pluto cries, "Sic semper tyrannis! Kill him that you may live!" But Neptune whispers, "Submit! Remember, the meek will inherit the earth. A savior is coming to deliver you!" Uranus cries, "Know the truth, and the truth will set you free!" But Neptune beckons, "Come into my grotto! I'll make pearls of your eyes and coral of your bones, and it won't cost you a nickel!" Pluto says, "Change, or you will die! Even you are mortal, and so are all your works!" But Neptune answers, "Don't believe him! I have plenty of pie for you in the sky—all you have to do is come and get it!"

A true revolution can never get off the ground without the aid of Neptune, the ruler of the powerless, the oppressed, the enslaved, the pariahs, the misbegotten, and the afflicted. The enlightened, reformist zeal of Uranus will amount to only an intellectual wind unless the hopeless children of Neptune can find one of their own, a human materialization of their dreams, to lead them. All the aggressive violence of Pluto will never make a revolution by itself. It will remain mere gangsterism until one gangster, like Adolf Hitler, emerges from the mob and starts talking with the tongue of Neptune, promising salvation to all who follow him.

The hypnotic power of Neptune is so great at certain times that when large numbers of helpless people realize they have come to the end of their endurance, they "play seize on any available man to serve as their savior. By the power of their collective, but unconscious will, the speechless put the words they want to hear into his mouth. The sleepers, collectively dreaming the same dream, transfer the sense of it to him, so that it becomes a compulsion he must act out before their eyes. Do they follow him, or does he follow them? It is an occult question, one of the mysteries of Neptune, the lord of the occult. The only certainty seems to be that when enough men in the same predicament strongly feel the need of a savior to rescue them, a savior will appear. Or someone appears who will serve the purpose long enough to excite the emotions of the helpless so that Uranian or Plutonian rebels can count on their support for the revolution, and also count on them to make massive sacrifices to achieve it.

The support of the Neptunian masses consists of passive acquiescence in the drift of events, bolstered by faith in the charismatic leader. Faith in miracles is part of the savior syndrome of Neptune. It must be so because these are *helpless,* powerless people, weighted down—perhaps for centuries—with a conviction of their own inadequacies. As long as the Neptunian leader preaches that their faith will make their dreams come true, they will stick together to provide the Uranian intellectuals and the Plutonian warlords with cheap labor and cannon fodder. When the Neptune leader dies, the emotional euphoria he excited evaporates. The unity of the Neptune movement disappears almost overnight. Petty leaders who want to step into the great man's shoes divide the mass into factions. The broken dream ends in a nightmare of tribalism, heresy wars, and witch hunts.

If the civilization is very old when the Neptunian revolution occurs, like India, China, or ancient Rome, it may never recover. Internal dissension and fragmentation will make it a prey to invaders, who will conquer and destroy it. Foreign barbarians will enslave the children of Neptune, but their unrealized dream will not be forgotten. It will be incorporated in a religion the conquerors may well adopt, and the story of their dreamlike struggle will be told over and over in myths, fairytales, and the sagas of saints.

If the civilization is comparatively new and internally vigorous, like modern America or Europe after the crusades, Uranian groups or Plutonian tyrants (sometimes both) will weld the fragments together from within the society. Then, in time, miracles will begin to happen for at least some of the oppressed. But they will happen only for those who cease to feel helpless, for those who detach themselves from the conforming mass of dreamers and begin to act as individuals with some personal, inner planet goal. For the children of Neptune, salvation begins when they cease to believe in saviors, when their misery becomes a personal rather than a collective problem, when they cease blaming others for their plight. Above all, when they stop *wanting to suffer.*

Masochism is the monkey on Neptune's back, and he keeps it there by telling his dreamers, over and over, that there is merit in misery. In the Neptune creed, all of your suffering is *somebody else's fault*. You are guiltless of responsibility for the horrors of a world you did not make. But do not complain, do not resist. The more "they" exploit and mistreat you, the greater their load of guilt and sin becomes. And surely someday, promises Neptune, you will be saved and "they" will be damned. The miracle will happen, and you will have the unspeakable joy of watching your enemy squirm. Just remember that you are Cinderella, the only waif in the world whose tiny foot will fit the glass slipper the Prince is carrying around in his pocket. If not in this world, then in heaven—think of the ecstasy of watching your enemy burn while you pluck your harp! Or, if you've lost your faith in heaven and hell, believe instead that you will get even with your tormentors in your next incarnation. It's a promise, says Neptune. All you have to do to earn these glorious rewards in the hereafter is to go on being a martyr now.

Unfortunately, Neptune never keeps his promises. That is why his genius and great insights usually end up mortgaged to Uranus and Pluto.

Let us consider some of the qualities of Neptunian leaders, which they all share. They have a romantic, other-worldly orientation, an avowed lack of interest in the things of this world. This may be carried so far among the early Christians and Buddhists that it amounts to lack of interest in continued life on this plane of existence. St. Paul thundered, "Then let this mortal put on immortality! Oh grave, where is thy victory? Oh death, where is thy sting?" The early Buddhists rejected the Hindu concept of reincarnation as a condemnation to the hell of eternal recurrence. They sought annihilation of the self in Nirvana. Rousseau and Gandhi advocated escape from this world by a retreat into a simpler, more primitive past, where everyone would live close to nature like a "noble savage" (Rousseau), or support himself by primitive handcrafts symbolized by the spinning wheel (Gandhi).

Hitler was not a Neptunian leader, but a Plutonian tyrant. Yet he preached the Neptunian retreat from the present to a more romantic and simpler past, where the old Germanic virtues would once more be in the Ascendant, the Teutonic knights would prevail, and every German would be a Siegfried or a Brunhilda. Hitler was born with the Neptune-Pluto conjunction in Gemini. Many of his contemporaries who had this aspect also used Neptunian arguments to achieve Plutonian ends, especially those who were prominent leaders in the socialist, communist, and anarchist movements.

The Neptunian leader advocates passive resistance: "Render unto Caesar the things that are Caesar's; render unto God the things that are God's." But their preaching against violence has the curious result of inciting to violence for which the leader disclaims any responsibility. Martin Luther, who went around exhorting the peasants to resist the superstitions and exploitation of the Church, is said to have been horrified when they rose up in armed rebellion against it.

There is always a race, class, religion, or system that must be made to seem guilty of all the miseries and frustrations from which the followers of the Neptunian leader suffer. This race, class, religion, or system must be made to realize its guilt and atone for it endlessly. Unfortunately, the strange irrationality of Neptune sees to it that no confession of guilt, no amends, no reparations, are ever sufficient to pay off the debt. Neptune cannot forgive because the enemy is the symbol of some force, power, virtue or achievement the followers of Neptune want desperately, secretly admire, and wish in their dreams that they had, or were. One of the psychological quirks of Neptune is that it wants to be something other than itself, but the something it wants to be is impossible for it to achieve. The mechanism is to make someone else guilty for what I lack, cannot do, cannot have, cannot be; or even, as in the case of Nazi Germany, for a defeat Germany suffered in a war Germany started. The transference of guilt from the weak to the strong is a most pernicious, masochistic lie and no matter how often it is told or how many scapegoats are sent to the guillotine, the masochist will continue to search for someone to abuse him. Killing kings and aristocrats has never yet magically transformed the rabble into a company of noblemen. Instead, the sudden absence of masters always sends the masochists into the streets screaming for a new tyrant, preferably one of themselves who will understand their need and wield a bigger whip with a crueler hand.

The Neptunian leader preaches the doctrine that his followers have a cosmic right to be taken care of. They are told that if they do not work, refuse to cooperate with the system or with those who are guilty of causing their misery, the system will automatically collapse. They have the moral right to refuse to help those who persecute them, but they also have the moral right to be fed and cared for no matter what happens to the system. They band together in cells, communes, monasteries, racial enclaves, and share what they have in brotherly love. They work sporadically at crafts not associated with the system, and they live by begging, petty thievery, and handouts from the guilty. They want but little here below, but they want that little continuously, as penance from the guilty for their suffering. In the system the Neptune leader promises his followers, everyone will always have everything he needs without having to work. Such work as must be done will seem like play. After all, the argument goes, we are only miserable outcasts because the guilty exploiters who run the system have hogged everything (the fruit of *our* labor). But it's a rich world, and once we take it over by means of our passive resistance, there will be enough for everyone to live on forever in innocent simplicity. As long as the Neptune leader keeps talking, it never occurs to any of his followers that the wealth they covet is part and parcel of the system they want to overthrow. When the system goes, the wealth it engendered will go with it, and, there won't be enough for anyone, let alone for everyone.

Communism is a Neptunian economic theory.

Finally, the Neptunian leader is a martyr. If he isn't actually assassinated, like Gandhi and Martin Luther King, he is constantly persecuted. This is essential for success in the role. The leader must take on the Establishment without flinching, knowing that his acts will lead to prison, torture, even death. He must nail his theses to the church door; he must travel all over the Roman Empire making incendiary speeches against the authorities; he must encourage his followers to lie down in front of trains so that the British cannot govern India; he must incite judges to fury and policemen to mayhem. *He must suffer in public.* His martyrdom has no effect upon the Establishment. Actually, it may hinder the achievement of the revolutionary goal. But the martyrdom is not assumed for the Establishment, not even to increase the sense of guilt it should properly feel.

His martyrdom is solely for the benefit of his followers. He is the projection in the flesh of their will to suffer, and they can only believe in the dream as long as they can see, with their own eyes, the triumph of masochism and passivity over everything else.

A curious feature of the Neptunian psychology and pattern of action is that it cannot succeed without the cooperation of another group or individual who is willing to accept responsibility for the miserable condition of the suffering group or individual. In the revolutions where Neptune's tactics succeed, there is always a fairly large element of sympathizers and fellow-travelers who belong to the system that the oppressed have vowed to overthrow. These people accept the accusation of guilt leveled against them and support the Neptune leader and his revolution with money, hard work, and propaganda. They pity the oppressed, they want to right the wrongs their ancestors did, they accept blame for social customs and conditions they had no responsibility for and which may even have passed away long before they were born or occurred in a strange land or culture. We all know cases of this phenomenon. Many Americans borrowed guilt for the miserable condition of the Russian masses under the Tsars, although neither they nor their ancestors had ever been near Russia. Or there's the case of the European who emigrated from Europe in 1920 whose children accept the guilt for black slavery in America.

To succeed, the Neptunian leader must solicit these converts who, through a vague, unfocused sense of pity try to atone for crimes they did not commit. For one thing, they bring him some of the resources of the enemy: money, publicity, arms, and shelter; sophisticated, professional advice; legal and medical help. For another, they are saboteurs (Neptune) in the enemy camp to which he and his followers do not have entre. On the psychological plane they are invaluable because, since they are from the enemy camp, they can always be blamed for anything that goes wrong and, in extremity, executed for it. Their constantly reiterated *mea culpa* proves that the children of Neptune never can be held responsible for anything they do or for anything that happens to them. Also, the converts are usually more belligerent and openly aggressive than his natural followers can afford to be. So, while the leader preaches nonviolence, the converts can go out and incite to violence, thus teaching the meek the most ancient of all methods to inherit the earth.

The only Neptunian leader who openly admitted to being a masochist was Jean-Jacques Rousseau. He was born in Geneva on April 6, 1670. Since the hour is unknown, the chart given here is of the Johndro type.

Rousseau's revolutionary activity was entirely intellectual. He was one of the founders of the Romantic Movement that fostered concepts and ideologies of the Neptunian type. He was actually a sophisticated, middle-class intellectual who would have been quite miserable and unable to function in the sort of world he advocated as the ideal environment for man. This was a world of noble savages living on roots and berries in an idyllic wilderness where all men loved each other while reposing on clouds of unshakeable goodness. With true Neptunian idealism, he avoided traveling to Plymouth Colony or Jamestown to see what life in the Wilderness among the noble savages was really like.

In his most important book, *The Social Contract,* he stated the thesis that a just society must be founded on a freely entered contract between the governed and their governors. Although this concept is basic to the idea of democracy, Rousseau was more a socialist than a democrat. Capitalism was practically nonexistent in his day (he died long before the Industrial Revolution), yet his work is clairvoyant in its romantic loathing of everything capitalism later came to mean: it is almost as if he knew what Marx would say two centuries before Marx said it. Going through time in the other direction, most of the ideas of the young hippies were first stated by Rousseau, although probably few of them have ever read him. He never actually fought in any revolution. Words were his only weapon. Yet few men in history have ever marshaled so many revolutionary troops behind them, or, years after their death, toppled so many crowned heads. It would be difficult indeed to overestimate his importance.

The first thing to notice about his chart is that the Sun, although strong by sign in Aries, is unaspected except for a semisquare to Saturn. The Sun symbolizes our concept of our own worth, our self-respect. In the charts of masochists it is often unaspected, in a sign of service like Virgo or Pisces, or in adverse relationship to the Moon or Neptune. The effect of such conditions on the Sun is to make individuals feel vaguely unworthy, inadequate, because little that happens to them or little that they do seems to make a favorable impression on others, or on the world. The Sun in square or semisquare to Saturn is not, in my opinion, an indication of masochism. It does indicate a hard struggle to achieve recognition which may contribute to a sense of worthlessness if other factors in the chart show a tendency to masochism Sun square Saturn is the indicator of a self-made person, and the semisquare, although far weaker, probably means the same thing Rousseau was certainly self-made.

In Rousseau's chart, the Johndro Ascendant opposes a conjunction of Saturn and Uranus in Pisces, the sign of suffering that is ruled by Neptune. I interpret this to mean that Rousseau often felt a compulsion to denigrate himself and to seek punishment (Pisces) for some nameless guilt

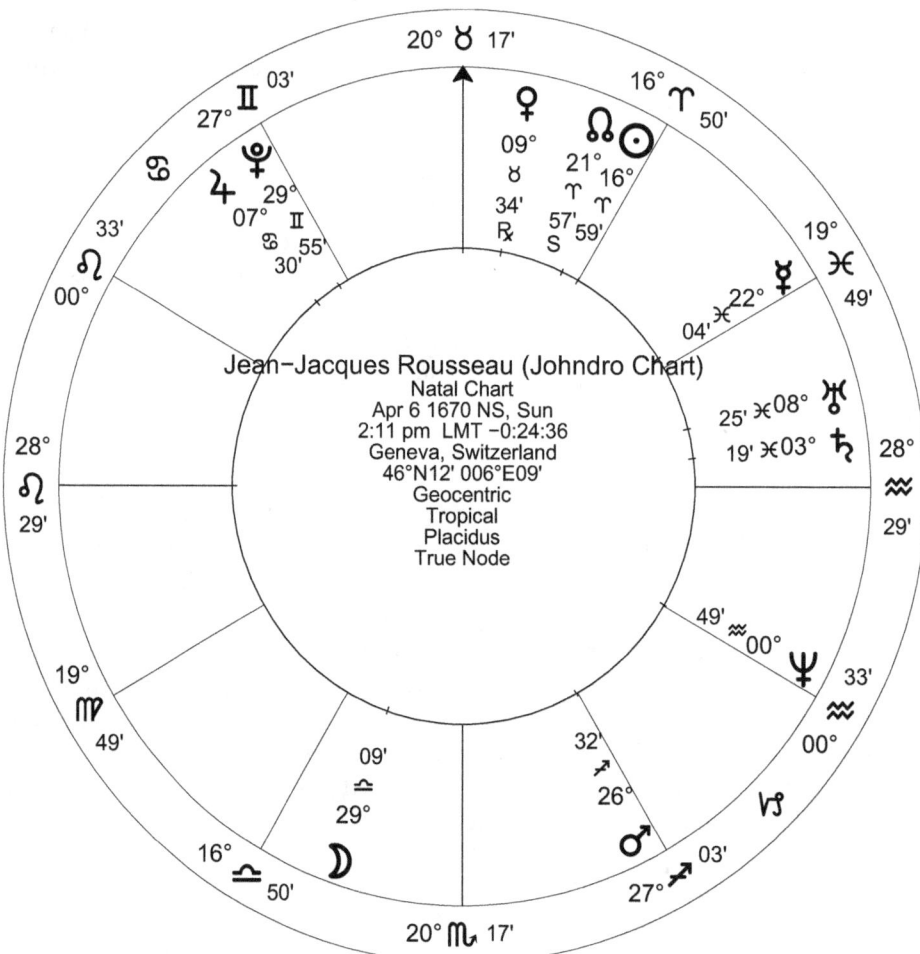

(Saturn). Yet, because Leo was rising, he had plenty of conceit and sought to overcome his inner feelings of worthlessness by dramatizing himself, not always truthfully. Self-dramatization is a quality of Sun in Aries, while Leo simply dramatizes everything. But any man who calls his autobiography his *Confessions* is both masochistic and conceited.

In the charts of masochists, the Moon and Venus are usually unafflicted by the aggressive planets, and may be, as in Rousseau's case, beautifully aspected by them. The Moon and Venus are significators of women, and masochists are not aggressive toward them. In fact, like Rousseau, they usually seek to be dominated by women, or dominated by another man through a homosexual relationship. Here the Moon is sextile Mars and in a grand trine to Saturn and Pluto. Its only affliction is the ego-crushing square to Neptune. As for Venus, it dominates the Johndro chart and is in a double sextile to Uranus and Jupiter.

Considering the far-reaching revolutionary effect of Rousseau's writing, the mutual reception between Uranus and Neptune is interesting. The revolution he advocated was of the romantic, impractical, Neptune type. What he got, long after his death, were revolutions of the Uranian type. His first rebel child was the United States, born with Uranus exactly on the Ascendant. The American Constitution is the first historical realization of Rousseau's social contract. The French Revolution was his second child. Uranian revolutions are usually fought against kings to achieve parliamentary representation for the people. Rousseau had to wait until 1917 for his Neptunian child to be born, in Russia. Neptune's revolutions are usually fought for racial, class, or economic reasons, and democratic government does not result from them.

The persistent immortality of Rousseau's ideas and the tremendous historical impact they had after his death are indicated in the Johndro chart by the grand trine involving Pluto, the significator of immortality, or fame after death; and by the fixed stars: Regulus is on the Ascendant, Fomalhaut on Saturn, and Markab on Mercury, all stars of great importance for fame.

Like many masochists, Rousseau was a fetishist. Fetishism is a Neptunian aberration because it displaces erotic attention from the sex organs to some part of the body or even to some object that normally does not excite sexual interest. Rousseau's fetish was female buttocks and thighs, indicating latent homosexuality and erotic fixation on being whipped. He also wanted women to trample on him (foot fetishism), as one might expect from the two malefics in Pisces (the feet) opposing the Ascendant. Saturn signifies being trampled on, or pressed down by a great weight.

I have gone into such detail to describe the action of Neptune in society and history because here, at least, we can all see its mode of operation and its results. In the private lives of ordinary individuals, Neptune's effects are by no means so clear. People who suffer from Neptune's afflictions seldom know what ails them or what really motivates their actions. The astrologer should remember, when confronted with difficult, puzzling oases, that Neptune acts in private life exactly as he does in public life. Do not assume because Neptune afflicts an inner planet in a chart that the individual is necessarily dishonest, a deliberate liar, or engaged in fraud. He is more apt to be innocently deluded, natively sincere in his belief in lies told by other people, or else the victim of shell games rather than their perpetrator.

Inner planets adversely affected by Neptune indicate areas of self-deception or impotence, or affairs that have a strange tendency to disintegrate. Where Neptune afflicts, the things or people signified may be idealized, even worshiped, but at the same time there is a perversion of values, a distortion of reality, about those things or people. This is why, in sex, Neptune rules fetishism, for that aberration is actually an idealization of some non-sexual object and the distortion of its prosaic utility into an erotic symbol. Worshiping this symbol has a disintegrating effect upon the sexual capacity of the individual, rendering him impotent in normal sexual situations.

For instance, where Neptune afflicts the Moon in a male chart, as in Rousseau's case, there may be a tendency to idealize women (as he did) to such an extent that they symbolize mother-goddesses for him. A mother-goddess is so exalted and sacred a being that her male worshiper cannot possibly insult her by making love to her, so he becomes impotent in her presence. The whole relationship is removed from a sordid, earthly plane to a romantic, heavenly one. Such a man claims he is "unworthy" to kiss his mistress's foot, and is quite unaware that he is telling the world he is a masochist and a foot fetishist. Or that those who hear him will be more apt to think he is ill than to think he is noble. But that is the way Neptune works.

Those with Neptune afflicting the Moon, regardless of their sex, are prone to idealize the common people (the Moon), to work for Neptunian causes, to follow Neptunian leaders, or to seek friends and associates the rest of the world considers inferior to them. Such people may make great personal (the Moon) sacrifices (Neptune) for the poor and unfortunate. An extremely powerful Neptune that has hard aspects to the other outer planets but does not seriously afflict any of the inner planets may also cause a person to idealize the common people or to sacrifice a great deal to try to help the poor and unfortunate. In such cases, however, the individual is not motivated by unconscious masochism. There is no desire for self-annihilation or confusion about sexual orientation, and the individual does not cop out into the salvation syndrome. Such a person may actually be painfully realistic, even clairvoyant, about the problems that face him or the world, and his clairvoyance (Neptune) may make him pessimistic about his chances of success.

Karl Marx had a chart of this type. Uranus and Neptune were both in the tenth house of career, in the sign Sagittarius. Aquarius was rising, with both Saturn and Pluto intercepted in the Ascendant in Pisces. Saturn was square Uranus, and Pluto was square Neptune. None of the inner planets are afflicted seriously by this massive double square, although Venus is in a separating quincunx to Neptune. This is not enough to warrant a conclusion that his sexual orientation was abnormal. He did suffer political persecution (Saturn rising in Pisces) for his revolutionary ideas (square Uranus) and had to flee to a foreign country (Uranus, chart ruler, in Sagittarius of foreign lands) to pursue his career (tenth house). The quincunx between Venus and Neptune seems to describe his quarrel with his wife's family, for Venus rules her house of money and resources. Her family was comparatively rich, but they disowned her for marrying a Jew and preferred to let her and her children starve rather than send her money as long as she stayed with Marx. This may indicate that he was selfish in exploiting her love for him (Pluto rising sextile Venus) but not that his relations with her were sexually aberrant. There seems little doubt that Marx and his wife were devoted to each other, and what little joy they found in a life full of tribulation may well have come from their love.

Never conclude that because the three outer planets are adversely involved with each other and with Saturn that the person is sexually perverse or aberrant. Adverse aspects between Uranus,

Neptune, and Pluto last for from five to ten years and their involvement with Saturn for a year or more. Clearly, many thousands, even millions, of people are born all over the world while such aspects prevail. These aspects have great social and political significance in the fate of nations, and the generations born while they prevail will be more actively involved in the wars, revolutions, and changes that occur as a result of them. A man may *live* in violent times without being violent himself. Or he may live in times like our own when all forms of sexual aberrancy are advertised as better, more exciting, and more desirable than normal expressions of *love,* yet never succumb to the propaganda.

The outer planets describe social conditions and world events over which we have no control. If an individual's inner planets make no contact with the outer planets, he may remain untouched, even unaware, of the most devastating social upheavals. A reincarnationist would say that in the present life he had no karmic connection with them. Or, as in Marx's case, the inner planets may have largely favorable connections with them. Then his involvement with the troubles of his times will be to his advantage; he will be aware of the social problem, but as an observer rather than as an active participant. Or, if he becomes actively involved, the choice freely made for personal and usually realistic reasons. Only where the relationships between inner and outer planets are strong and stressful does the psychological pressure from the outside world become too strong to resist. Even then, the individual's adjustment to them may be constructive and lead to important work, as in Rousseau's case.

During Neptune's fourteen-year transit (1956 to 1970) of the sign Scorpio (sex), it was in sextile aspect to Pluto (sex). Part of this time it was also sextile Uranus (liberation, rebellion), and for about a year it was also trine Saturn (constraint, discipline) in Pisces (punishment, the payoff). Neptune always subverts the values of the sign it transits. It brings those values to the forefront, but in a confused, distorted, deceitful and *idealized* manner. It offers us a brand of poison of the nature of the sign it transits and seduces us into drinking it by telling us this is the medicine that will cure all our ills. Trines and sextiles are soft, permissive aspects that no one tries to fight. The result of this combination of outer planetary influence was a flood (Neptune) of pornography over the masses (Pluto), deceptively presented in the guise of enlightenment (Uranus). We were all urged to try communal orgies (Pluto) and to experiment with sadism, masochism, homosexuality, and anything else we could think of without Saturnian restraint or inhibition. Uranus and Pluto were in Virgo, the sign of analysis and health. So the news of the sexual liberation was brought to us in how-to books and movies analyzing sexual techniques in the detached style of technical manuals (Virgo), and seeming to show great concern for our health and well-being. Even the authorities (Saturn) succumbed to the wave of sexual permissiveness, and in many Western countries the laws against pornography were repealed.

As Neptune moves into Sagittarius, the whole thing will be revealed for what it actually was: a strange delusion and crowd madness like a sexual version of the Tulip Craze (1634 to 1637, when speculation in tulip bulbs caused an economic crash felt throughout Holland) or the Mississippi Bubble. It is not repressive law or censorship that will kill the pornography mania, but a sudden, overwhelming, collective boredom with it. Nothing is so boring as prolonged permissiveness or so dead as one of Neptune's delusions when the dream is over and the sleepers suddenly awake.

Impotence

Neptune's mode of action in sex, as in everything else, is of the type that psychologists call "passive-aggressive." It is the technique of the drunkard, the dope addict, and the hypochondriac. Neptune rules alcohol and drugs, including poisons. During Neptune's over-permissive passage through Scorpio, these people have also been idealized and romanticized. They have become the beneficiaries of much official charity and tender-loving care. Alcoholism was judicially proclaimed an illness and clinics were set up at the taxpayers' expense to cure it. The junkie has been declared a "victim of society." It's the old Neptune trick of forcing the innocent to accept the guilt and with it the responsibility for someone else's inadequacy.

Drunks, drug addicts, and hypochondriacs are Neptunian cop outs who somewhere along the line have refused to both wake up and to grow up. They are indeed ill, but their illness is the Neptunian *will to impotence*. Their passive-aggressive message to society is that of the child who's been punished for his naughtiness: "I'll go out in the garden and eat worms, and then you'll be sorry!" The response of the wise parent is to give him a trowel and an empty coffee can to help the project along.

Neptune is the lord of impotence, whether this manifests physically or psychologically. Impotence is Neptune's weapon both of defense and of domination, just as the knife is the weapon of Mars, charm is the weapon of Venus, words of Mercury, guns of Uranus, bombs of Pluto, the cudgel of Saturn. Those who are legitimately helpless, like the truly ill, the very young, or the very old do not come under the rulership of Neptune. They all have a valid claim to care and attention until they get well, grow up, or die.

All societies that are in a healthy phase of development or in a stable period recognize this and automatically take measures, through customs established in culture and morality, to assure that the temporarily helpless will not develop the Neptunian will to impotence. They achieve this with a minimum of fuss and expense simply by giving everyone who needs help some socially valuable task to perform commensurate with his strength and experience. This fosters the sense of responsibility and self-respect in the temporarily helpless and discourages the growth of the desire to use helplessness as a weapon over others. Self-respect, ruled by the Sun, self-reliance, ruled by Mars, and the acceptance of responsibility, ruled by Saturn, are the antidotes for Neptune's poison: the will to impotence.

The overprotected child who is told he's too *little* to do anything *useful,* too ignorant to experiment with anything, or too stupid to know what he's talking about has no yardstick by which to measure the rewards of self-respect and self-reliance against those of self-denigration and helplessness. He develops the will to impotence because he's been trained to believe that he can't do anything worth doing; so why try? Since the only rewards he has ever known are those gained through helplessness, and no one wants to live all his life without rewards, he naturally cultivates the passive-aggressive method of the helpless to force someone else to take care of him.

The passive-aggressive technique dominates others through weakness. It is a malicious, underhanded power game that subtly subverts the slave and the master, the sick and the well, the criminal and the jailer. Who is more ill, the masochist who says, "Trample on me!" or the sadist who does the trampling? The drunk who goes on a binge every time something hurts his feelings, or his wife who sticks around because "she doesn't know what Harry would do without her?" The kid who takes dope to get even with his parents for not letting him grow up, or the parent who kept him cooped up in a play pen as long as possible and then sat him down in front of the boob-tube for hours on end "to keep him quiet?" The habitual criminal who only feels safe in jail, or the society that can't find anything useful for him to do when he's penned up? In the fog that Neptune makes of all values, nobody knows.

Every astrologer who practices for very long soon accumulates large files of the victims of passive-aggressiveness and the will to impotence. The recognition of Neptune at work comes quickly, and it is rapidly followed by realization that passive-aggressiveness and the will to impotence are Neptunian forms of sexual fulfillment. The commonest case is that of the drunkard and his long-suffering wife. She is the client. Upper middle-class, well dressed, refuses to admit that she came because she has a problem. "I just came because I was curious," she says. "Mary Jane Brown said you were very good." But she does have a problem, and the chart tells what it is. The astrologer says, "You're thinking of leaving your husband, aren't you? Just can't take any more of his drinking. Is that it?"

Her defenses crumble and the story pours out: Married twenty-five years; he's wrecked the children's lives and hers; every time he gets the family in some humiliating mess, he swears he'll never take another drink; once he stayed on the wagon five years—he really *does* try; then our daughter Sally got married, he got drunk at the wedding, made a terrible scene; now he's drinking at work. I go every night to pick him up because I'm afraid to let him drive; I don't want to leave him—he's such a wonderful person when he's sober, and very talented, really brilliant; if only I could get rid of the feeling that it's somehow my fault! He never drank before we were married. He started after Johnny, a sickly baby, was born, so I didn't have much time for Harry. I got the feeling sometimes he was *jealous* of his own son! I know I can't take any more. Every time we go out, he humiliates me. If I try to have people in, he manages to get blotto before they come. I've been on the point of leaving him a dozen times, but something always stops me. I just can't bear to think of what will happen to him if I'm not there to protect him."

And they haven't had sexual intercourse for years because Harry can't quite manage it. He's either out cold or he laughs and says, "I guess old John Barleycorn is getting even with me for giving him up."

The truth is that Harry is getting even with his wife for having another baby when she should have known *he* wanted to be her only baby. Now Harry is fixing it so she'll always have to take care of him whether she likes it or not; he's going to see to it she has to pay more attention to him than to that other baby. If she thinks he's going to make love to her, she's crazy; doesn't she realize he's punishing her? Harry has gone out in the garden to eat worms because his mother (wife) let him down. But with Neptune canniness, Harry *did* pick the right wife. She was the only one out of all the women he knew, perhaps, who wouldn't lock the door on him and let him eat worms to his heart's content. It is a marriage made in Neptune's peculiar hell. She'll never leave him, and he knows it; because just as he gets his kicks from being impotent, she gets hers from keeping him that way.

The pervasive use of drugs among the young began when Neptune was in Scorpio under permissive aspects from Pluto (sex) and Uranus (rebellion). In the usual Neptunian fashion the drug culture is idealized by those who belong to it and regarded with horror by those who don't and yet accept the guilt for it. As with other Neptunian phenomena, both camps agree as to the cause, which is not social injustice or persecution this time, but "alienation." It is not actual, legitimate alienation, like that of a stranger in a foreign land or culture, a member of a minority race, or the genius whose insights are ahead of his time. It is emotional alienation stemming from a strong feeling of personal inadequacy.

Orphans, unwanted people, and illegitimate children are all ruled by Neptune. Neptune also rules damaged goods—that is, junk. (It is curious how aptly slang sometimes picks up astrological meanings and imbeds them in the language without anyone knowing they are astrological. Heroin is "junk"; the heroin addict is a "junkie"; cocaine is "snow"; LSD is "acid"—all ruled by Neptune.) To an outside observer of the drug culture and the hippie movement associated with it, the most striking, peculiar aspect of both is that the participants are not orphans, outcasts, or illegitimate children. They are the carefully nourished, usually spoiled children of over-indulgent, middle-class parents most of whom, because of the Depression and World War II, had a rather hard time and wanted to spare their children the painful experiences they had themselves. Unlike black ghetto children or the children of many immigrants in earlier periods, those who join the drug cult are not the offspring of alienated parents, but of conformist, hard-working people, respectable pillars of society. That, these children of Neptune will tell you, is the whole trouble. They are alienated because their parents aren't. They feel a strong compulsion to punish their parents for not being alienated, and at the same time they want to atone for the sins of their parents' complacency.

The morality of the hippie movement requires its participants to reject all the values, comforts, traditions, and protections of the permissive society in which they were reared. The first step is often secret experimentation with drugs. This is an unconsciously motivated attempt to force the parents to reject the child overtly (transference of guilt). Very few parents do this, however. They accept the guilt, try to atone for it, and smother the child with all the benefits of psychiatry. They do all the same things they've always done to make him realize he is the center of their universe, and that he alone matters; and all they ask is to be loved, just a little, in return.

What they don't realize, and what the child doesn't realize either, is that love is a cooperative adventure, a give and take proposition that leads to mutual enchantment. No one who is trained from infancy to believe that he is the center of the universe can grow up capable of feeling love. All this child knows is that when he yells, his parents hop; when he says "gimme," they give; when he gets into trouble, they get him out of it. He is the emperor who can do no wrong; they are the slaves who tremble before him, kowtowing whenever they see him. How can he possibly love them? Or anyone? Who could possibly be worthy of the love of such an exalted being—except, of course, himself.

So he leaves home, partly to punish them by his absence, partly in search of the Holy Grail. Somewhere in the wide world there must be someone he can love, some cause worth serving, some savior who will rescue him from the deadly boredom of being the center of the universe. Like Haroun al Raschid, he puts on the disguise of a beggar and lives like an orphaned outcast on handouts, while he searches through forbidden alleys for something that will turn him on. All he finds are others like him, wearing the same clothes, talking the same language, motivated by the same impulse, sharing the same communes. He finds a strange exhilaration in being part of a crowd, in chanting with the others at festivals and demonstrations: it makes him feel a diffuse warm glow, as if he finally belonged somewhere, was part of something, and the drugs, of course, turn him on. Unfortunately, even though a group gets stoned together, each trip turns out to be a lonely adventure in a private, psychedelic world.

Each participant in the movement goes to a great deal of trouble and endures many sacrifices to play the role of self-made orphaned outcast. He will have the image, if he cannot have the fact. He is anxious for the world to know what it feels like to be unloved. He talks of almost nothing but peace and love. Like a lonely old maid, he cherishes stray cats and dogs and takes them to bed with him for warmth and comfort. He holds hands with strangers and takes his clothes off in public so that more of his flesh can touch more of theirs. Everywhere he goes he has a childlike faith that someone will take care of him, that someone will love him, enough to give him a quarter just for doing his thing.

After a time, he begins to acknowledge that he feels a deep, growing resentment against the world, which isn't hopping when he screams. It both refuses to love him and refuses to listen to him. The world he wants to influence and reform is the one he came out of. As is the habit of worlds, it accepts the image (Neptune) he has made of himself as the reality. It finds him dirty, scabby, selfish, parasitical, the sort of person only a mother could love. And it's not terribly interested in watching him do his thing because (another habit of worlds) it's quite busy doing its own.

The hippie drug culture is a movement composed of a myriad of people who believe they are the center of the universe, who come and go and touch each other in the dark. They are inwardly ashamed of being incapable of love for another human being because that is the mark of psychic impotence. Drugs accomplish two things: they give a temporary illusion of ecstasy, and, if you take them long enough, they make you physically impotent. When that day comes, you can stop searching for love because it's obvious you couldn't do anything with it if you found it.

The sexual symbolism behind the hippie drug culture, where every center of the universe is doing his thing, is masturbation. Each of these children of Neptune is Narcissus, forever admiring his own image in the pond, his back turned to the world.

Chapter IX

Pluto as a Sex Significator

Violence and Delinquency

Pluto rules the three great mysteries: sex, death, and reincarnation. They are closely connected, and one cannot be understood without consideration of the others.

Sex, death, and reincarnation came into the world together as a triad of necessity. Although we may choose to interpret this symbolically on any plane of knowledge or existence, it is also a fact of the natural world which would be true even if no human beings existed on earth to interpret anything. The earliest forms of life were sexless (pre-Plutonic) and immortal. The amoeba grows by cell division to an optimum size; then splits into two parts. Not only does it never die, it also never attains individuality—each one is an exact replica of all the others. Primitive plants like algae do the same thing. Among creatures, worms are as high on the evolutionary scale as this process goes, although some egg-laying reptiles are able to grow new tails if those they were born with are damaged.

Next in the evolution of sex come the spore-bearing plants like ferns and fungi. Ferns have sterile fronds and spore bearing fronds on the same plant. The function of the sterile fronds, which are larger and tougher, seems to be to protect the more delicate fertile fronds until the spores mature and dry out sufficiently so that the winds can carry them off to plant them in a distant place. The new ferns so propagated are exactly like the old ones. But even at this early stage of sexual development, death enters the life chain because the parent fern may die, although probably not from natural causes. By which I mean they probably do not have a natural, preordained life span like more highly evolved forms.

Sexually differentiated plants and creatures come next. In species like the holly, the gingko, the ailanthus, the male and female trees have a different appearance. Only the female bears fruit or seeds, but there must be a male tree somewhere in the vicinity for this miracle to be accomplished. Bees are not necessary for this type of propagation; the wind will do. This is a method full of risks; not only because the individual trees are mortal and propagation depends upon a series of accidents, but also because there is always a remote chance that an accidental hybrid may be created, a different individual, with a slightly different appearance and habits. Many sea creatures propagate in a similar way: the female lays millions of eggs, the male may swim over them and fertilize them. Again, the method is hazardous and relies heavily on fortuitous accidents. But it is a sexual process, and the parents are mortal. The young are individuals, and there is always the possibility that one of them may be slightly different from the others.

Sex begins to get intimate among the social insects, and with intimacy there suddenly appears a sharp taboo against promiscuity. There is only one fertile female in a colony, the queen. She is created by feeding her special food. At the proper time, she leaves the hive or colony, selects a male to mate with, then he dies, his sole function fulfilled. The rejected males lose their fertility and become drones, miserable, hardworking slaves who live but for a season. Here, for the first time, is sexual intercourse in the true sense and it proves a hazardous adventure for the male.

The insect colony in the natural state is so inbred that one individual is not distinguishable from another except by specialized function. There is no chance for new types to occur through mongrelization, because the queen must inevitably breed with one of her offspring. Any new queen created through feeding a larvum the right diet will also be one of her offspring. This clamp down on promiscuous sex was probably nature's way of sealing off the insects from further evolutionary development; it may indicate degeneracy. The insects may be changed, however, by mutation caused by something in the outside environment suddenly affecting them.

By the time we reach the birds, mammals, and hermaphrodite plants, sex becomes a strong biological drive, so strong that promiscuity within the species is controlled only by natural limitations upon the length of the breeding season. In nature, birth control is biologically enforced upon all animal species that propagate by sexual intercourse. Otherwise the animals might propagate so vigorously that their environment would soon be unable to support their numbers, and the entire species would die of starvation. Only man, with his arrogant contempt for nature, thinks he can indulge in all the sex he wants without practicing any kind of birth control and still survive.

Our present population explosion is a Plutonian phenomenon. Having made some progress in the conquest of death (Pluto), we have disturbed the natural balance between life and death by which, in former times, the weak, the malfunctioning, and the overly greedy were eliminated in large numbers. But death is so intimately connected with sex and so necessary for the process of evolution through mongrelization and hybridization that Pluto will avenge himself in countless mysterious ways, which we cannot foresee.

Now the outermost planet, Pluto has replaced Saturn, Uranus, and Neptune as the final arbiter of law from which there is no appeal. The law of Pluto is unpleasant: it is that of the dictator, the gangster, the warlord, and he dispenses it in a kangaroo court always rigged against the defendant. We have upset the balance of nature by abusing the environment and by begetting more people than the Earth can support. Pluto will stop at nothing to right the balance. Total war, atomic war, famine, genocide, riots, gang and street crime, anarchy—all these are Pluto's death-dealing weapons. When the balance between life, death, and the life-sustaining environment is out of joint, any or all of them come into play. Unlike natural death, they are not selective. Everyone or anyone goes who happens to be in the path of destruction, except a lucky few who may come out of the holocaust damaged.

As sex evolves among the animals, various interesting things happen. The male and female sex organs become more and more differentiated in outward form, so that the sex of highly developed mammals can be known immediately at birth: the sex develops in embryo and is genetically determined. Secondary sexual characteristics become more and more marked: the brighter plumage of the male bird, the antlers of the male deer, the mane of the male lion, the tusks of the male walrus, the conspicuous mammary glands of human females, the growth of facial or body hair on white-skinned human males. The greater the differentiation between the sexes, the more selective and self-conscious the mating process becomes. Stags fighting over females, with the females electing to go with the winning stags, have come a long way from the fishes that never know their mates and fertilize any eggs they swim over. With increasing differentiation between the sexes, the number of young produced by any pair becomes smaller, and the length of infant dependency upon the parents increases. The normal life-span also increases, and the length of the period of fertility. The percentage of those born who survive to maturity increases markedly.

Among the animals, the ability to select a mate freely increases with mobility. The farther an animal can range, the greater his chances of selecting a mate who is slightly different from himself. Perhaps it is only a difference in the color of her fur, the shape of her nose, or the kind of foliage she can eat. Every child of the union will be a new individual, different from both parents, yet the reincarnation of both because he will carry the genes of both. Reincarnation does not mean that we are immortal, like the amoeba; it means that we will be born again and again in a new body. As the Baghavad Gita says, bodies are like suits of clothes: we discard the old ones to put on new ones.

The Baghavad Gita is talking about the reincarnation of a non-corporeal entity that never loses its individuality regardless of the number of times it changes bodies. But each new body brings new associations, new experiences, new lessons, and new knowledge. Each incarnation supposedly enriches the soul and increases its freedom to choose what kind of body it will put on next. The rich man has many garments to choose from before he dresses to go into the street; the poor man has but few and they may all be rags. Through his freedom in the choice of garments, the rich man may go many places and do many things: suitably dressed, he may join the hunt, attend the ball, travel abroad, and be welcome among kings, scholars, soldiers, sailors, merchants. In the same way, the enriched soul has great *mobility.* Like the poor man, with his one threadbare suit, the undeveloped, inexperienced soul is welcome only among others dressed like itself.

It is the same in the biological sphere of sexual development. The greater the mobility of the animal, the greater freedom he has in his choice of a mate. Each such outbreeding within the species increases the diversity of the genes in the offspring, until finally it becomes impossible to predict whether the new kitten will be born wearing white, black, tan, grey, yellow, striped, spotted, or calico fur; whether it will be long or short, flat or fuzzy, coarse or fine; whether its tail will be long, short, bushy or sleek; whether it will be sweet-tempered or nasty; a fighter or a coward; a good mouser or a bad one. Because of the far-ranging mobility of its ancestors and their renowned sexual promiscuity, each kitten born has a rich genetic wardrobe to choose from. And each emerges as a distinct individual different from the others in the same litter and different from all its ancestors, as its descendants will be different from itself.

Genetic development (enrichment) occurs through mongrelization of animals and hybridization of plants. Any great degree of mongrelization is possible only among creatures that can move about in comparative freedom and are thus exposed by accident to chance encounters with others of their species slightly different from themselves. The more complex the genes, the more improbable it becomes that any individual in the species will be exactly like any other. In human beings, with their extraordinarily complex genetic structure, it is literally impossible to produce a child who will not be an individual. Therefore, when the genes of the parents are reincarnated in the child, the new garment those genes will put on is chosen from a wardrobe of almost infinite size and scope.

It is not possible for us to know the purpose behind any natural process. But from what we know of the effects of mongrelization, hybridization, mutation, and the forced adaptation of creatures to changes in their environment, it seems probable that the purpose of sex is the achievement of *individuality*. Sex is the biological force through which the process of individuation occurs. It is not necessary for survival: the sexless worms and amoeba survive more persistently than any sexually differentiated species except the insects that eternally duplicate themselves. Sex is necessary for the achievement of variety, variety is necessary for the achievement of complexity, and complexity is necessary for the achievement of individuality. It is *only* through the process of individuation that evolutionary development can occur.

But sex is impossible without death. The process of individuation will not work automatically unless the sexually differentiated individuals in the species are allowed some freedom in their choice of mates. They cannot be given this freedom and also be allowed to prolong their individual lives unduly. No individual can be allowed to choose the hour of his death because individuality is an arrogant condition of being. The individual, in his uniqueness, is an egotist. To desire immortality is a failing of arrogant egotism. Were we able to achieve it, there would soon be too many of us for our environment to support. Then the process of individuation would slow down because crowding decreases mobility and the danger of starvation increases conformity. As the environment becomes impoverished, the creatures it has to support become impoverished. Their sense of adventure narrows down to the search for the next blade of grass, the next grain of rice. They are beggars again, with nothing to choose from but a wardrobe of rags.

Pluto rules sex, death, and reincarnation. And because he rules all these, he also rules the process of individuation. The sexual aberrations symbolized by Pluto's afflictions to inner planets are connected with death, violence, and the necessity to prove that one is an individual who can dominate other individuals.

Rape, as a form of sexual fulfillment belongs to Pluto. The compulsive rapist cannot attain full physical satisfaction from a consenting partner or from a prostitute, both of whom willingly participate in the sex act. For him, euphoria followed by a sense of well-being comes only from brutally forcing another to submit to him and usually injuring her in the process. Satisfaction comes more from the domination of another than from the sex act itself.

Rape is an extreme form of physical self-assertion. It is usually perpetrated by people who belong to a race, age group, or social class that feels itself inferior to some other race, age group, or social class. Often the rapist has himself been subjected to brutal treatment by his father, a gang leader, a tyrannical boss, a prison guard, a foster parent, or an orphanage keeper. Such cruel, dictatorial figures are Plutonic types who become symbols of the dominant race, age group, or class which, through force and cruelty, makes the oppressed person feel helpless and insignificant. He feels that he has been deprived, through force, of his right to become all individual. He begins to suffer psychologically from a ghastly compulsion to prove to himself and others that he is not an insignificant nonperson. He will force "them" to notice him, even if he has to kill one of them to do it. But killing in itself is not enough, nor is it always necessary! What is important, what alone can bring the deep inner contentment he seeks, is the forced submission of another person who represents or symbolizes the hated race, age group or class.

Rape is an act of symbolic vengeance (Pluto). The ideal victim represents the oppressors, but she is always a weak or helpless member of the oppressing class. She must be caught unawares, alone, attacked from behind, in the dark, and yoked or beaten so that the rapist runs no risk of being humiliated by resistance he may be unable to overcome. The habitual rapist is so profoundly convinced that he really is a nonperson that he dare not attempt to assert himself as an individual against anyone who might remind him of this fact, even by a word. That is why so many women who resist rapists are killed. It is also why rape so often becomes a compulsive, uncontrollable act: it never really achieves its goal, which is to make the rapist feel like a man instead of a worm.

Child molesting is also a Plutonic sexual aberration, for the same reasons.

Pluto is the significator of great wealth. As ruler of Scorpio, it symbolizes other people's money. Many Plutonic aberrations mix up money and sex in a peculiar, muddled way. Other people's money may become a fetish—that is, something that induces sexual excitement. Obtaining it through violence, particularly with a gun (a phallic symbol), then becomes a symbolic sex act, a symbolic rape. The rationalization is much the same as with the physical rapist. He who feels like a nonperson tells himself that money will make an individual of him. But he too is a coward. He selects an unarmed victim, frequently a woman or a drunken man. Banks, those guardians of other people's money, are prime targets for the postgraduate operations of this type of robber. Banks are a uterine symbol; robbing them is symbolic rage.

People who suffer from an undeveloped or inadequate sense of individuality frequently band together in gangs (Pluto) and commit both sex crimes and robberies collectively. A characteristic of gang operation is extortion through torture. Here, the connection between money and sex is obvious, because all torture is an expression of a sick sexuality.

The sex orgies which became so fashionable while Neptune was in Scorpio are also a Plutonic phenomenon. Any illicit, undercover, illegal *group* activity connected with sex, violence, or money comes under the rulership of Pluto. So does juvenile delinquency. This is an attempt of the young, through lawlessness, to dominate the mature and to take vengeance upon them for their "oppression" of the individuality of the young. Juvenile delinquents, whether they come from ghettos, suburbs, or mansions, feel that they are nonpeople, that their right to become individuals has somehow been stolen from them. And one must admit that in many cases it has been.

Astrologically, the most interesting and complex cases of Plutonic afflictions occur when two people are compulsively united in a love affair through close ties to Pluto between the two charts. Then, after coming together, they commit murders in cooperation, although before they met, neither was violent.

A case of this sort is that of the Moors murderers, Ian Brady and Myra Hindley. The charts of each, considered separately, are innocuous; Brady's is actually weak and ineffective. When superimposed, however, the two charts become a vicious unit.

The closest Plutonic bond like this in my files is that between Bonnie Parker and Clyde Barrow, the trigger happy bank robbers of the 1930s who left a trail of death and violence through the dreary little towns of Texas and the Midwest. Considered separately, each chart is violent and unfortunate. Both have an exact square between an inner planet and Pluto. In Bonnie's case, it is Mercury, ruler of her solar ninth house of law and her solar twelfth of outlawry. In Clyde's case, it is Venus, ruler of his seventh house of marriage and his second of money. When they came together in their compulsive love, Bonnie was the one more victimized by the affair, for her Venus falls in close opposition to Clyde's, and square to his Pluto.

Karmic connections, or karmic fate, are shown by planets falling in the degree of the Moon's Nodes. Both these charts have the Nodes in the same degree, 21 Taurus-Scorpio in Bonnie's case, and 21 Gemini-Sagittarius in Clyde's. Bonnie's volatile T-square between Neptune, Jupiter, and Uranus falls in 21 Cancer, Libra, Capricorn; and Clyde's Uranus is also in 21 Capricorn.

These two not only had a gruesome karmic connection with each other, but also with society. Because *outer* planets fall exactly on the degree of the Nodes in both charts, they felt personally injured by the society in which they had been born. The extraordinary, mindless fury of their revolt, and its absolute futility, indicate that their grievance against society was a psychic carry-over from another, more primitive period. When compulsive action leading to self-destruction emerges as the life pattern, the astrologer looks beneath the surface meanings of the chart for an explanation, just as the psychiatrist would look beneath the surface consciousness of the mind for one.

The psychiatrist finds his explanation in the personal psyche. The astrologer finds his in the eternal psyche, or reincarnating psychic entity. This is especially true when two people are compulsively bound together, like Bonnie and Clyde, with karmic aspects between the two charts. Exact Nodal connections with planets are karmic.

The Sun in a woman's chart in close major aspect to a man's Saturn indicates a burden of responsibility carried over from other lives; here the aspect is an opposition, which usually means that only death will break the bond, however irksome it may become. The man's Moon on the woman's Saturn (here a conjunction), indicates the same thing, and frequently denies surviving children to the union. I believe that this aspect, if connected with the eighth house (as here) indicates that the couple killed or brutalized their children in previous lives; and that now their relationship to society is similar to what was once their relationship to their children—brutalizing and murderous.

Mutual relationships between Venus and Pluto are sexually compulsive: Bonnie and Clyde had been lovers many times before, often in illicit relationships that brought death to the woman, as once more, in this life, it brought death to Bonnie.

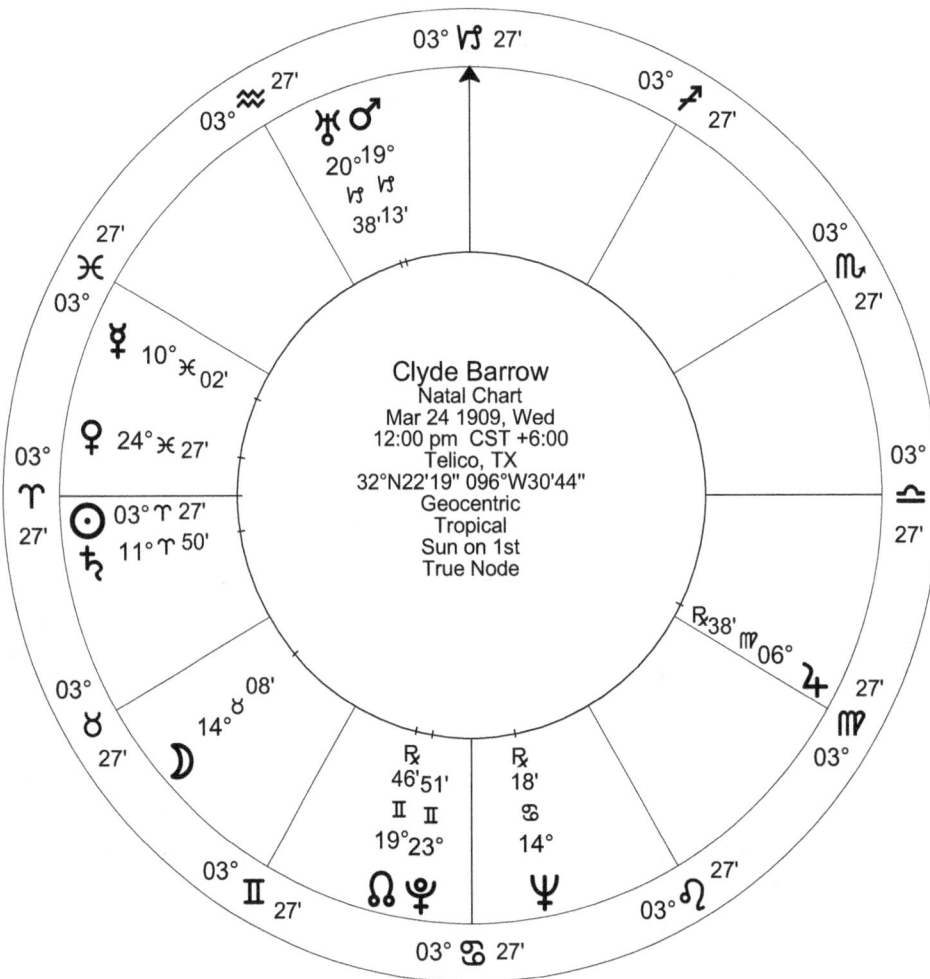

Bonnie's Mars opposition Clyde's Saturn is an aspect of willful violence. If the Sun is also involved (as here), it indicates that the person with the Mars-Sun conjunction (Bonnie) once suffered death by burning at the hands of the other, or through his fault. Because Bonnie's conjunction is in Libra, the sign of public executions, I think she was once burned at the stake for heresy. (Jupiter square Uranus is a mark of the heretic—one who does not conform to the ideologies of his society.) Karmic memory of such a horrible death at the hands of another society may help to account for Bonnie's psychic grudge against the one she attacked at gun-point in the 1930s. In this one, too, she was executed in public, shot down in a blaze of bullets by the police.

It is not possible to investigate esoteric astrology (the theory of karma) scientifically with the tools now available to us. But I usually try to ask clients born with Sun conjunction Mars in ad-

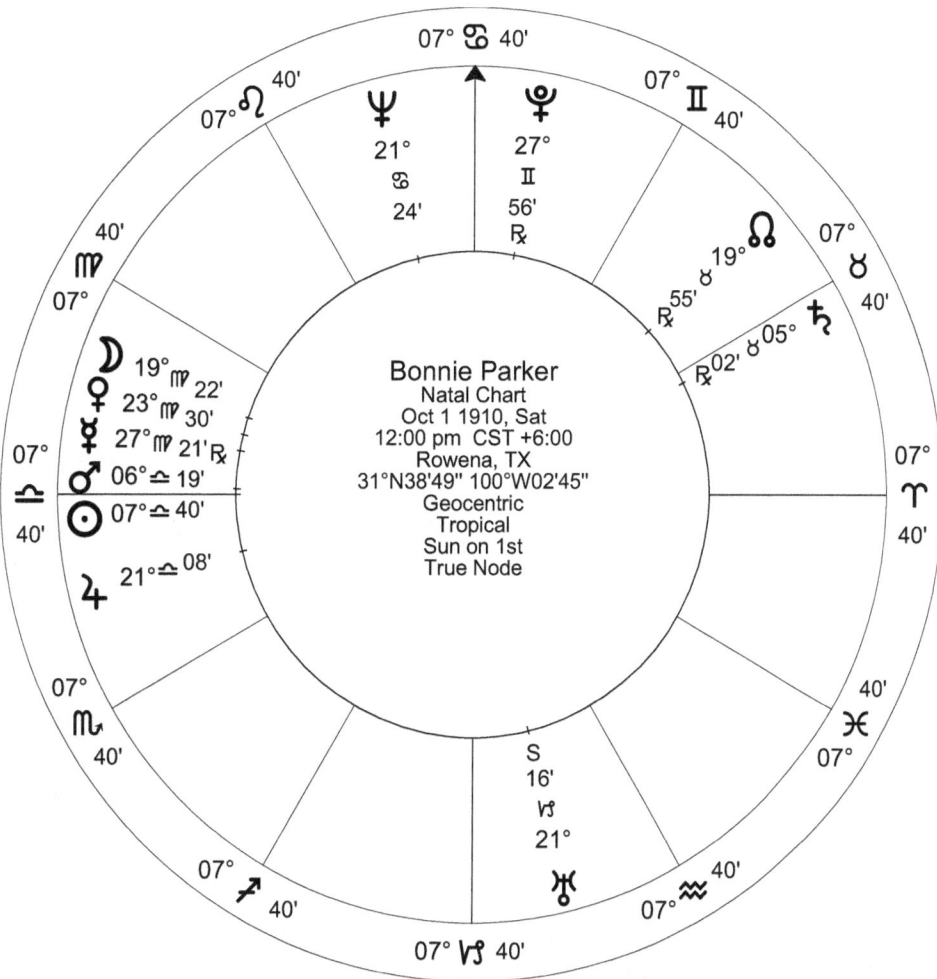

verse aspect to Saturn how they feel about the Middle Ages. They respond with expressions of revulsion against the period. Some say it makes them ill just to read about it; some say that Gothic architecture depresses them. One said that in his childhood he had always associated burning leaves in autumn with the Middle Ages, he could not imagine why, and the smell of the smoke always made him sick. One said that when he was in the army in Europe he always felt a terrible sense of desolation when he found himself in one of the open squares before a cathedral, although he had gone to the town specifically to see the cathedral, and he somehow associated this sense of desolation with the Middle Ages.

Perhaps people who were once burned at the stake never get over it, however many lives they live thereafter.

The romantic version of Bonnie and Clyde presented in the movie is far from the truth. They were two harried people who were sexually excited by danger. They found exhilaration in violence and an orgiastic pleasure in being chased, and this was connected with a triumphant sense of power whenever they succeeded in stealing other people's money. In many years spent studying and practicing astrology, I have examined thousands of charts. I cannot remember any worse than these two, any more willfully destructive.

Rape

Rape is the commonest sexual aberration of Pluto. According to his own confession, Albert DeSalvo, who also claimed to be the Boston Strangler, raped hundreds of women over a period of many years. Probably he exaggerated. He was born with Mercury trine the Moon, the aspect Charles Carter stated was the mark of a liar; but, as I have said before, I find this to be a certain judgment only when one of these planets aspects Saturn adversely. Here both Mercury and the Moon trine Saturn, but Saturn also afflicts the Moon with a contraparallel. However, there seems to be no doubt that DeSalvo did rape a great many women. He was tried for this offense and convicted of it on the testimony of several who identified him. He has never been tried for the strangler murders because, for one thing, there seems to be no evidence against him except his own confession, and under present American law a man cannot be convicted solely on the basis of his confession.

But there is no doubt of his aptitude as a liar and dissembler, for he usually gained access to his victims by getting into their apartments under false pretenses. He exploited a mild manner, an inoffensive, respectable appearance, and a sharp ability to quickly analyze a situation. These are all characteristics of Virgo, where he has four planets. Even at the height of the strangler murders, when the women of Boston lived in terror, DeSalvo was able to get into their apartments by pretending to be a repairman who looked neat, seemed disarmingly helpful and quite harmless. Virgo has a genius for neatness and helpfulness; its ability to blend unnoticed into the background of any environment is phenomenal.

He also had a photographic memory, which we can explain by the Mercury-Sun conjunction trine Saturn. It is alleged that in his confessions to the murders he described details of the various apartments, which he had never seen before or since, and which he could not have learned from reading accounts of the crimes. He also described many circumstances known only to the police.

On the surface it appears that the worst thing about DeSalvo's chart is the grand cardinal cross between Pluto, Mars, Saturn, and Uranus. While this is certainly a difficult and dangerous configuration, we have to remember that it lasted a long time and many people were born with it who never committed rape or murder. That doesn't change the fact that the configuration is potentially dangerous and violent. It would be interesting to know what percentage of those born

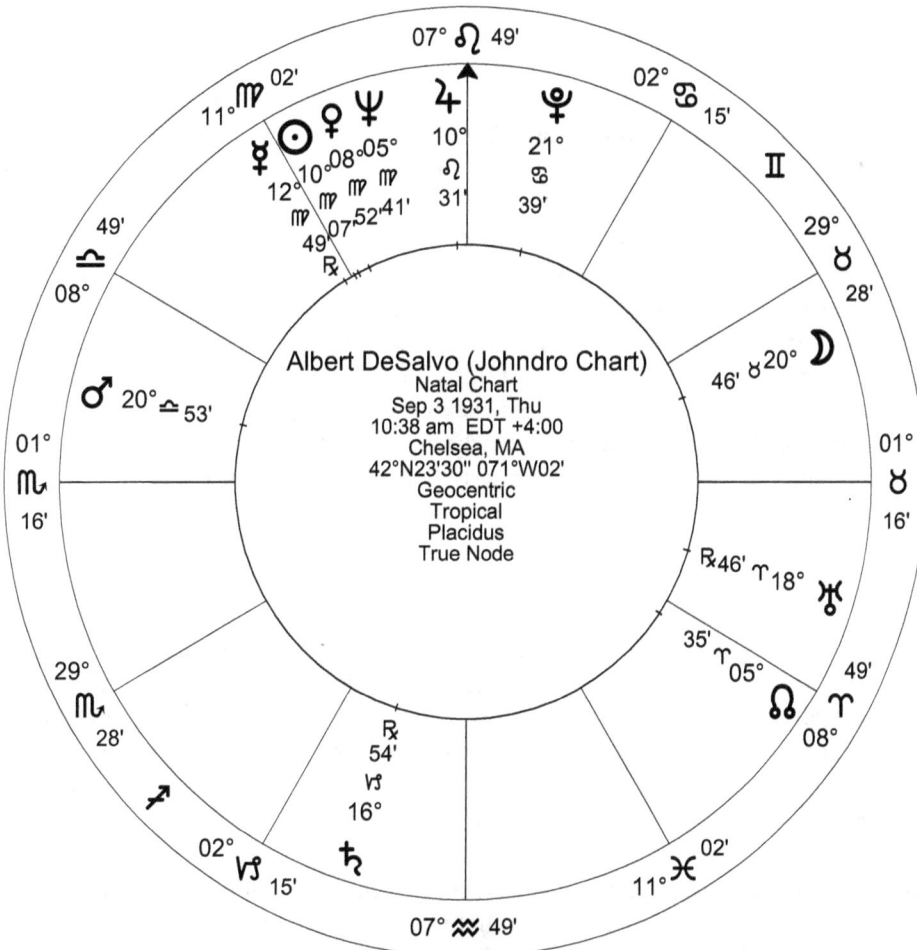

with it, throughout the world, survived the anarchy, revolutions, and tyrannies of the 1930s, the German and Russian concentration camps, and World War II. Not many, I should think.

To explain a career like DeSalvo's, which revolved around sex and was very harmful to women, we must look to the Moon and Venus. If we consider merely the zodiacal aspects of these planets in longitude, they do not seem to be under great tension. Venus is conjunction Neptune, Sun, and Mercury in the sexually inhibited sign Virgo. The conjunction with Neptune is certainly not good, especially in Virgo where both planets are badly placed. Any planet conjunction Neptune suffers from a perversion of its values: DeSalvo suffered from delusions about women and felt strange compulsions in regard to them. He is alleged to have said that he felt he had a *right* to sex, to all the sex he wanted, and that no woman had a *right* to refuse him. When one did, or when one *turned her back to him,* he felt an overwhelming compulsion to rape or kill her. Here again we see Neptune's mania for transferring guilt for all one suffers to another, innocent person. Usually, however, this conjunction manifests as masochism rather than overt sadism, especially when it falls in Virgo or Pisces, the masochist signs. There is one clue to the direction the perversion might take: Venus and Neptune are semisquare Mars, with Neptune being but eight minutes of arc from the exact aspect.

Now consider the zodiacal aspects of the Moon. It is trine Saturn, semisextile Uranus, sextile Pluto, and in a wide separating trine to Mercury. The only stressful aspect is a quincunx (150 degrees) to Mars. But remember that DeSalvo's hour of birth is unknown to me, therefore the chart given here is of the Johndro type. This aspect takes a narrow orb, so he might have been born at a time when it did not exist, although I do not think so. Quincunxes, especially if they affect the eighth house (as here) show maladjustment in sexual attitudes or in sexual capacity. Because of the circumstances of DeSalvo's life, particularly the brutal treatment he received in childhood from his father and the sordid misery of his early home environment, I believe that his cardinal cross fell in the angles.

It is the parallels that tell the story. The parallel is a close relationship between two or more planets formed in declination—that is, in their positions north or south of the celestial equator. When they are on the same side of the celestial equator, the parallel acts like a conjunction. When one is north and the other south, they act like an opposition. This is called a contraparallel. Parallels are probably more powerful than conjunctions and oppositions because they act more compulsively. They seem to operate in a fateful or karmic manner, through influences in the outside world that we cannot control, or through psychic compulsions that we cannot control either until we understand them.

In DeSalvo's chart, all of the inner planets except Mercury and Jupiter form parallels with one or more of the outer planets. The Sun is parallel Uranus: the outcast in rebellion seeking to express his individuality in eccentric or destructive assaults against the prevailing moral code. The Moon is parallel Pluto and contraparallel Saturn: morbid preoccupation with women, sex, and death. The contra-parallel to Saturn indicates an extreme sense of sexual privation or frustration. The parallel to Pluto solves the problem by illegal, violent, secretive domination through force. Venus is parallel Neptune and contraparallel Mars: delusions about women, which make them guilty of vague, inexpressible crimes against himself, for which they can only atone through sexual submission to his will. Mars is also contra-parallel the Sun (ego). This is an interesting complex, considering DeSalvo's sexual prowess. The contraparallel of Mars to both Sun and Neptune (which are not parallel each other) indicates a strong psychic sense of personal inadequacy, an all-pervasive inner conviction of impotence. Venus (women) mediates between these planets by its parallel to Neptune and its contraparallel to Mars, focusing the whole complex upon sex. DeSalvo felt inadequate in everything he ever tried to do, except during his service in the army (Mars), where he felt competent and appreciated. It was not quite enough to heal the psychic wounds of his miserable, brutalized childhood, however, for he claimed to have raped many women in Germany and near every camp where he was stationed. Still, he was almost happy in the army.

After he left it, he said in his confession, he lost all control over his driving need. It would assail him without warning, and his compulsion to satisfy it was uncontrollable. It was almost like a fit, except that every assault was executed with great care for details (Virgo). But no matter how many rapes he committed, he was never satisfied. The euphoria of relief lasted only a moment, then the pain of his compulsive dissatisfaction returned. So, he claims, he went on to murder. His relief after a murder lasted longer.

Ultimately, his whole career revolved around the manic necessity to prove that he was *not* impotent. He did not have to prove it to the world, but to himself (Mars rising). It was only after he was imprisoned for an unrelated crime and could not get at any women that he began to talk, thus reliving the proof of his potency.

Like many other sex criminals, he was aware of the compulsive nature of his need, and he was aware of it as painful. He wished, like so many others, that he hadn't had to do these things; and he always hoped in a vague, unfocussed way (Neptune) that someone would come along, or that something would happen to restrain him before it was too late.

Chapter X

Pluto and Genius

Sublimation of Sex and Violence

Rather late in his career Freud admitted that his psychoanalytical theory and method failed with two kinds of people: the psychotic and the genius. The confession was something of a Freudian slip of the tongue, for according to Freudian theory it revealed that in the privacy of his unconscious mind, he lumped the two types together as pretty much the same. So does very nearly everyone else. The conventional attitude of society toward the genius is that he is mad. The conventional attitude of the madman toward himself is that he is a genius.

The question, then, is: can the astrologer tell them apart? With our science in its present stage of development, I doubt it. Of course, if you hand an astrologer a dozen charts of geniuses, all carefully labeled by name, he will look for explanations of genius in the chart, just as Freud looked for them in biographies. Then, if you hand the astrologer a dozen charts of people with a medical history of schizophrenia, she will look for explanations of psychosis in them. But if you hand her a dozen charts without names, six of geniuses and six of psychotics, can the astrologer separate them? I doubt it.

You may ask if the astrologer can pick out anything very specific from an unidentified chart. The answer is that he can. Given a hundred charts identified only by sex, the experienced astrologer can flip through them and pick out those with a strong tendency to alcoholism, to homosexuality, to prostitution, to violence, to notoriety or fame, to business success or ultimate failure, to good or bad health, to a happy or miserable childhood, and so on. He can do this because all these tendencies are common in everyday life, and have been for centuries. Years of experience and study of historical documentation have established certain rules of judgment about any fairly common human condition. Just below the surface of his consciousness is a vast store of information, filed away. Never a day goes by when the practicing astrologer does not have to draw on this file, because every client he sees will have a chart showing tendencies to one or more of these statistically common human conditions. The client will either verify the diagnosis or point out circumstances that complicate or simplify the picture. This information too goes into the mental file, adding to its depth and meaning.

Some of these rules and patterns of judgment are so accurate that the astrologer can tell from them whether or not he has been given the correct hour of birth. Astrologer: "You had a miserable childhood, didn't you?" Client: "Oh, no! It was the happiest time of my life!" Astrologer: "If so, this chart is wrong and there's no use going any further with it." Client, embarrassed: "No, it's true. I was only trying to test you to see if you were really any good." That's like telling a doctor you have a terrible pain in your foot when what's really bothering you is a lump in your breast. It's your life you're playing games with, not his. And he's bound to find out, sooner or later, if only from the obituary columns.

Neither genius nor psychosis is a common condition. Most astrologers, if they practice long enough, have a few psychotic clients. But most will practice a lifetime and never encounter a genius. If, on the long chance, one did come in, the astrologer would probably think, "Now where have I seen something like that before?" Out of the mental file would come the few psychotic charts; not because they were *exactly* like the genius's but because they were more similar to it than to other charts in the mental file. If the genius said, "I'd like to know what my chances are to sell this gadget I've invented. Nobody will listen to me—they all think I'm nuts. Now the word's got round so they won't even let me in to talk to anyone. And I'm running out of money to go on to the next phase." The astrologer can see that this is indeed an inventive person, with a strongly emphasized third house, indicating powerful, but stressful problems there.

Well, what would *you* think if he was *your* client? If Pasteur ever went to an astrologer and said, "Look, I'm having a lot of trouble with my colleagues over this theory of mine. They're trying to kick me out of the university and destroy my laboratory. In fact, they're coming right out and saying I've lost my mind." Astrologer: "What's your theory?" Client: "Oh, I've discovered that germs cause disease." Astrologer: "What are germs?" Client: "They're invisible micro-organisms." Astrologer: "Monsieur, I think this would be a good time for you to take a long vacation in the south of France. You've probably been overworking. Rest, relaxation—they do wonders for—"

When he left, the astrologer would file his chart away with those others that were so peculiar they didn't fit anywhere, except together. So Monsieur Pasteur would rest in the file beside that poor man who died last year in the asylum, and that crazy painter who thought he could paint air, and that little spinster who thought she was the Virgin Mary, and that mad poet who wore an overcoat all summer, threw bricks into shop windows, and dyed his hair green—really, they should put him away! Too bad about M. Pasteur though—he'd really made quite a solid reputation for himself. But then, with such a weird chart, and all that stuff in Capricorn—undoubtedly delusions brought on by overwork. Perhaps, if he did take a nice long rest, but of course he won't. Who could rest with six planets in Capricorn?

What the astrologer does notice about both genius and psychotic charts is that they tend to be unbalanced: they often lack planets in one element or quality. They tend to have overstressed, usually afflicted, third houses (the rational mind); there is often a malefic in the third (Mars, Saturn, Uranus, Neptune, or Pluto), or the ruler of the third is in close aspect to one or more of these planets. The tenth house (career, public recognition, fame) is also often afflicted, and there is usually a close, stressful connection between the third and the tenth houses, indicating that the way the person's mind functions interferes with his achievement of a good reputation. The Ascendant is also usually afflicted: a malefic may be rising, or the chart ruler may be in close aspect to a malefic, indicating that the individual has personal difficulties in adjusting to society and may not be able to do so at all. There tend to be connections between the Ascendant and the third house, usually of a stressful nature, showing that these personal difficulties of adjustment come from the way the individual's mind functions, from his ideas and thoughts. For the same reason he has problems with everyday life, his neighbors, and in communicating his ideas to others—all matters ruled by the third house.

Mercury (the logical mind and the means of communication) is often afflicted by a malefic, frequently one of the outer planets. There are usually indications of sexual frustration, inhibition, or transference of sexual values upon other things; that is, a rationalization of sex drives, which makes them emphasize some nonsexual activity. Jupiter (success) or Venus (money) are often afflicted by Mars, Saturn, or Uranus, indicating that recognition of personal achievements is blocked, that the income is uncertain or nonexistent, and that the person gets money or recognition by unusual means, if at all. Finally, there is lack of concern for the individual's health, comfort, physical well-being that sometimes amounts to gross carelessness, as if he were deliberately sacrificing himself for some ideas, delusion, or work.

But there are two features of the charts of geniuses not often present in the charts of psychotics. The genius's chart is concentrated—what we call "tight"—showing a single-minded drive toward a specific goal. The psychotic's chart is apt to be scattered, diffuse, and directionless. Its afflictions pull him compulsively from one project or set of ideas to another, so that he never seems able to learn by experience, but always seems to be losing his way. The effect of the total chart is rather like that of a smashed bottle, with the fragments flying off in all directions. There is no gathering together of vital force for any battle that confronts such individuals, but rather a flight from challenge that in the end disintegrates the personality.

Pluto is usually strongly emphasized in the charts of geniuses, though not always favorably, through close contacts with the Sun, the Moon, Mercury, or the ruling planet. These contacts are often quite subtle, as with parallels, contraparallels, or mutual receptions. Pluto is the planet that rules *immortality,* and his presence in such powerful contacts is an indication of fame after death, however much misery they may bring during life. Of course, some psychotics also have strong Pluto contacts, as do Hitler and many famous murderers. In such cases, the meaning is the same: their reputations will survive them, and their infamy will assure their immortality. Sometimes a psychotic is also a genius, as in the case of Vincent Van Gogh.

In keeping with his theory that sex was the basis of everything, Freud thought that genius or unusual achievement was a sublimation of the sex drive. Certainly, in many charts of geniuses, sex is underrated, discounted, or the sex drive is simply weak, as in Rousseau's case, cited earlier. But the process of individuation (Pluto) has gone extremely far: geniuses are intensely individualistic. They are themselves against the world, which is why the world has so much trouble swallowing them. They are outcasts, because they think ahead of their times. They are future oriented, to a goal beyond this life. Instead of feeling the compulsion to create children to live after them, they create art, literature, inventions and ideas that influence future generations. Sometimes in looking at the charts of geniuses, I have the impression that these are often people who have transcended sex. They have found another, more significant route to immortality, which does not necessarily mean that they are sexless or sexually abnormal.

The three charts of geniuses given here were chosen because they were born about thirty years apart, thus the outer planets are not in the same Signs. They all had genius in different fields, yet each chart exemplifies some, or all, of the peculiarities mentioned above.

Pasteur

Louis Pasteur had an extremely unbalanced but very powerful chart. He had eight planets in the earth element and none in fire. Only one planet, the Moon, was in a positive (masculine) sign. This means he was abnormally introverted. Although he was apparently happily married, he was deficient in sex drive and was not aggressive. When his ideas or reputation were attacked, however, he fought back vigorously and courageously, for Libra, the sign of self-defense, was rising, with Ascendant square Mars. Most of his important work was done for practical reasons (Capricorn), and was commissioned by the French government or industrial associations. As one might expect of so many planets in Capricorn, he did not like to take chances with his income; he wanted to work for solid employers from whom he could collect his modest fees.

His first important work was on crystals: he formulated the laws of crystallization. Saturn and Capricorn rule crystallization. He discovered the principle of fermentation (Neptune), and saved the French wine and beer industry in a time of crisis by inventing his process of pasteurization, which stopped the fermentation at the proper point to prevent spoilage. When the

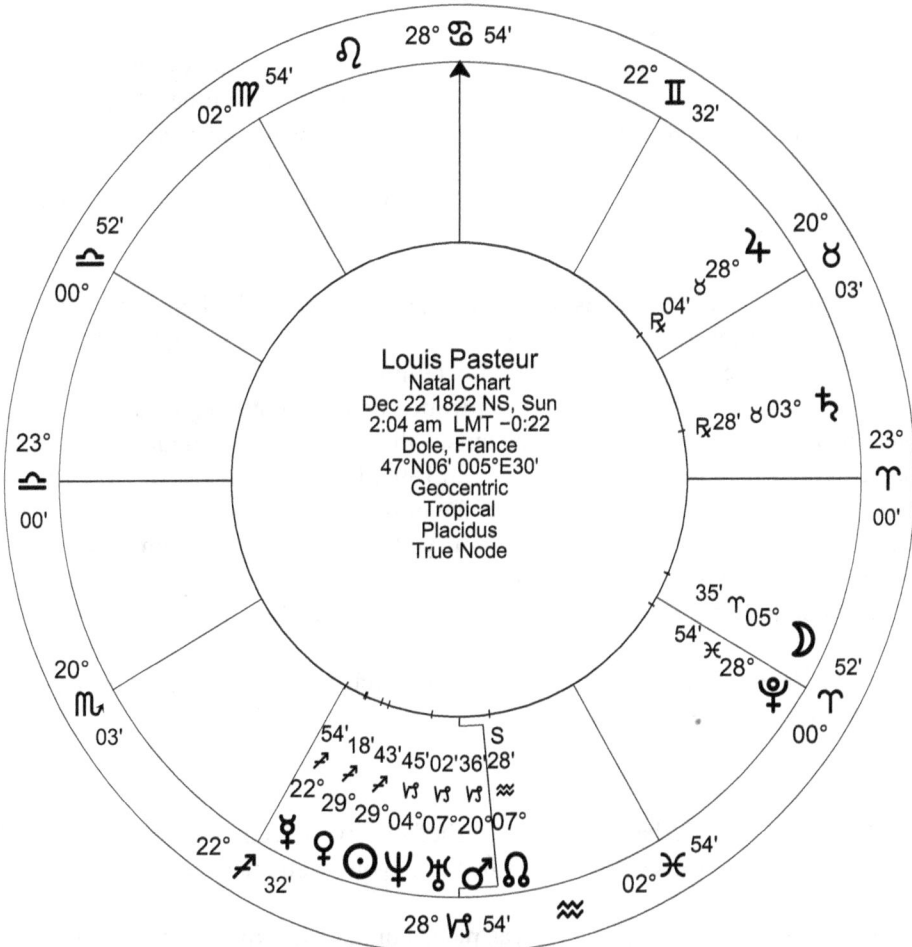

French cattle herds were threatened with extermination by anthrax, he isolated the anthrax organism and invented an inoculation to immunize the cows. Venus rules cattle, Neptune rules germs, and Uranus rules preventive inoculations—all planets in conjunction in the saving-of-wealth sign Capricorn, trine Saturn in Taurus, sign of cattle. He also saved the French silk industry by finding out what was killing all the silk worms. Venus rules silk, Neptune rules worms, Mercury rules spinning, and Saturn rules cocoons.

What excited the populace, the academicians, and the medical profession against him and nearly ruined his career were his announcement of his germ theory of disease and his discovery of an inoculation against rabies. This was the great controversy of his life, which he had to fight (Ascendant square Mars), but which he won with honor (Mars trine Jupiter). Mars rules rabies and rabid animals.

As for the aspects to Pluto: it is on the Pisces-Aries cusp, in square aspect (conflict) with the first five planets in Capricorn. Of course, Pluto was not known in Pasteur's lifetime, and Neptune was not discovered until 1846, twenty-four years after his birth. Another thirty or forty years passed before astrologers were certain it ruled Pisces, and even longer before they had much certainty of how it operated in the horoscope. If Pluto and Neptune are left out of Pasteur's chart, it would appear to be quite stodgy although, then, *two* elements would seem to be missing, making the imbalance even more acute.

To his contemporaries, and to any astrologer he might have consulted, he must have seemed a quiet, reliable, middle-class intellectual, a peasant who had come up in the world, but who had clearly got above himself when he insisted upon telling the August medical establishment what caused disease. Except for his work on crystallization and fermentation, whose value and originality were recognized by contemporary chemists, the revolutionary importance of his discoveries was scarcely realized until after his death in 1895. He was the father of the science of bacteriology. He invented antitoxins for some of the most terrible scourges of the nineteenth century: anthrax, diphtheria, tuberculosis, cholera, yellow fever, plague, and hydrophobia. Yet even now, in my 1962 edition of *Chambers Biographical Dictionary,* he is given only about half the space devoted to Boris Pasternak, who immediately precedes him.

Pluto is a planet deeply concerned with scientific research. It is the force that operates on human minds to bring the unknown to light.

Van Gogh

The next chart to consider is that of a very disturbed man who lived all his life under terrific tension from inner, psychic forces that neither he nor anyone who knew him could understand.

From the beginning, Vincent Van Gogh was placed under a disadvantage. He was born on the same day (March 30) and christened by the same name as an elder brother who had died soon after birth. As the living Vincent grew up he always felt that his family was making silent but undesirable comparisons between whatever he was and did and what the dead Vincent (now an angel) might have been and might have done. This shadow from the grave pursued him all his life with its ghostly reproaches, dooming everything he tried to do to failure. His Sun, ruling his third house of brothers and sisters, is within eight minutes of an exact contraparallel to Pluto, ruler of those who have died before us. His Mercury, symbol of brothers and in his own horoscope, ruler of the fourth house of the grave, was conjunction Pluto. As if this were not enough, Uranus, ruler of his own eighth house of death was also conjunction Pluto.

Once more we have an unbalanced chart, with the air element missing. The third house was afflicted by the Sun's contraparallel to Pluto, and although Mercury received trines from the Moon and Jupiter, it was in close parallel to Uranus, which in turn was parallel Saturn. Contrary

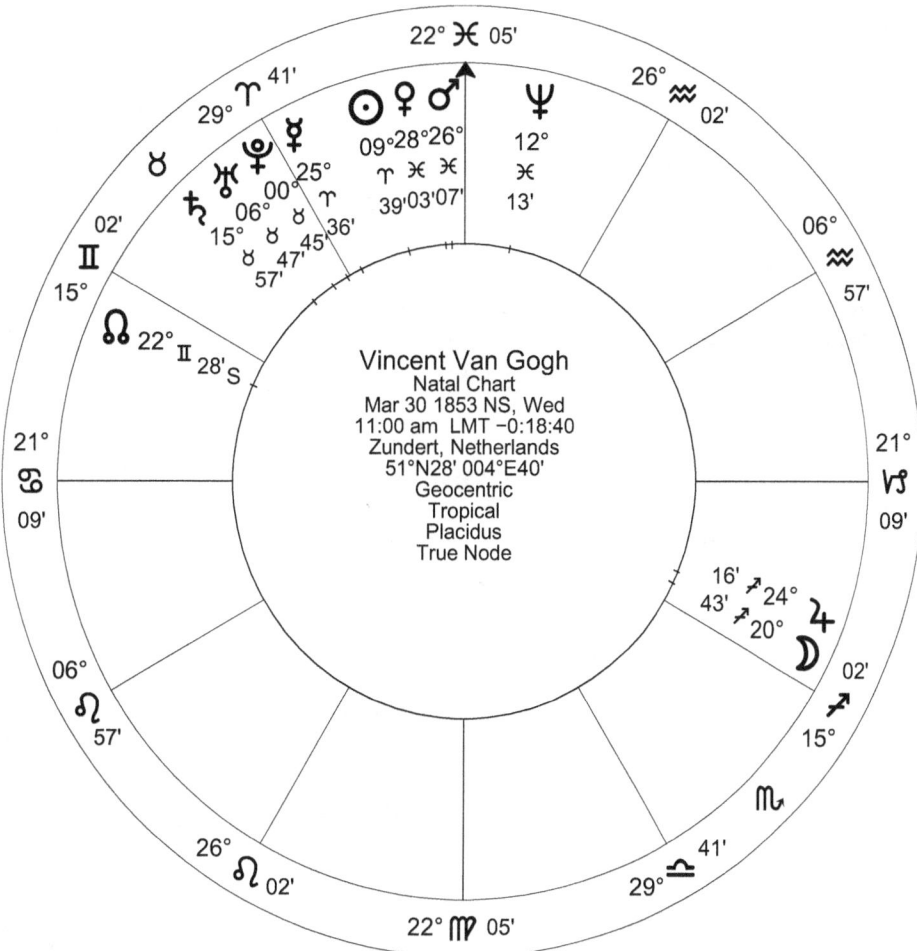

to popular opinion, trines to Mercury do not assure mental brilliance unless the outer planets are involved with them. Trines from the inner planets, especially from Jupiter, more often indicate an alert intelligent that readily adapts itself to conventional, popular thought and traditional standards of value. Time and again Van Gogh tried to do just that, but the parallel of Mercury to Uranus always spoiled his efforts, which ended in disgrace, quarrels, emotional crises, and broken health (Moon-Jupiter square Mars-Venus). Van Gogh had an enormous capacity for kidding himself about what he could and could not do (afflicted Moon trine Mercury). No matter what his fire-sign optimism dictated, he simply could not step into the shoes of his dead brother and fill them with honor; it was a standard impossible to meet. Uranus would always topple his tower of dreams with lightning suddenness, and, disillusioned, wrecked, he would run into hiding among the common people (Pisces), trying to find relief from his own shortcomings in the company of peasants, coal miners, prostitutes, and other outcasts (Jupiter square Mars).

The Uranus-Mercury parallel is interesting not only from the standpoint of the originality of his painting and the furious intensity with which he worked, but also from the standpoint of his mental illness. The aspect is nervous and impatient of constraint, especially when one of the planets falls in Aries. Mercury rules the logical thought processes, the nervous system, and those centers of the brain concerned with manual dexterity and words (speech). The sign Aries rules the brain as a physical organ. Uranus rules the circulation of anything, and therefore the circulation of the blood. When it is afflicted, especially by Saturn, as it is here through a conjunction and parallel, it is often the culprit in causing an incurable disease (Saturn), in which a microorganism or virus enters the bloodstream, circulates through the body, and eventually causes permanent damage to the bones (osteomyelitis and tuberculosis of the bone), the joints (arthritis), the nerves and muscles (poliomyelitis), the bone marrow (leukemia), or the brain (syphilis).

Although I have never seen this opinion expressed in any of the biographies I have read, nor in Van Gogh's own copious correspondence with his brother Theo, I believe from his chart that he contracted syphilis from the prostitute he married in The Hague. I think that he knew it, and that his necessity to keep silent lest he disgrace his family explained his sudden rages, his unpremeditated attacks upon people he loved, his spells of surliness, when he was unapproachable and actively nasty to everyone, his mutilations of himself (cutting off his ear to send to a prostitute), and his suicide. I think it also explains the passionate fury with which he worked during the last ten years of his life. He would have known he had not long to live. He would have known too that by contracting syphilis he had ruined forever any chance he might have had to surpass his dead angel brother in goodness. So he might as well spend the time he had left, before the darkness closed in, doing the only thing that had ever given him joy—and to hell with all the rest.

As a disease, syphilis is ruled by Pluto, which is here conjunct both Mercury and Uranus (the link between them) and is parallel the Sun, which in this chart is what we call *hyleg* (the life force or point of vitality). I do not think Van Gogh killed himself from any psychotic impulse to suicide. I believe that when he realized his sight was going, that soon the world of light he loved would be forever swallowed in darkness and he would paint no more, he took the pistol (Uranus) and blew his brains out (Mercury afflicted in Aries).

I also believe that the painting he was working on when he shot himself was an explanation of why he had done it—his suicide note to his brother Theo. It is a picture of a flock of hideous black crows in mad flight over a yellow field of wheat. It is a picture out of hell, a portrait of doom, darkness, desolation, and despair. It is the obituary of a soul in torment, dying of that secret (Pluto) scourge of the nineteenth century, which killed so many great men that it was christened "the disease of genius."

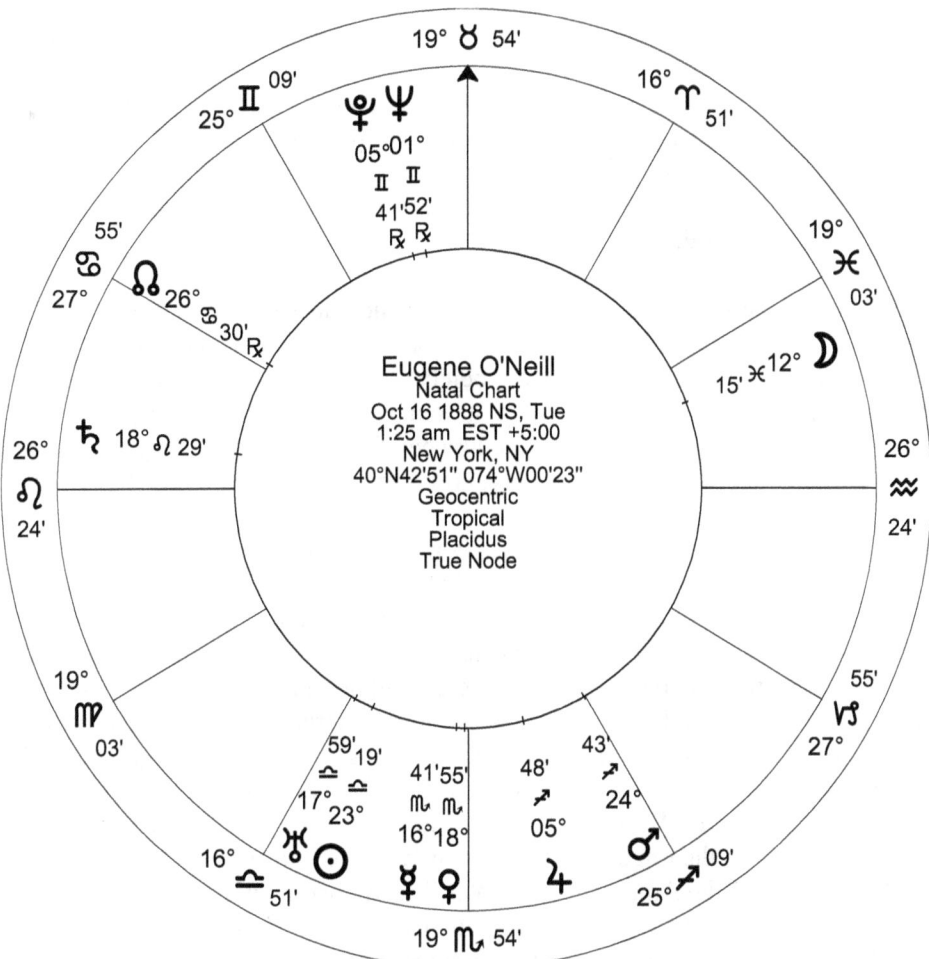

O'Neill

The last chart to consider is that of Eugene O'Neill. Once more we find that it is unbalanced, lacking any planet in the earth element. The third house is again heavily emphasized and afflicted by the conjunction of Uranus, with the cusp and the square of Mercury and Venus to Saturn, which in turn afflicts the Ascendant by its position close to the rising degree.

O'Neill was not one of the geniuses who suffered from lack of recognition during his life. In fact, he won the Pulitzer Prize many times and was the first American dramatist to receive the Nobel Prize. He also made a great deal of money from his plays. Yet, the strong emphasis on Pluto in his chart indicates that for all their popularity, his plays were not really understood either by the people who praised them or by those who scorned them.

O'Neill was popular with audiences, for he had the Moon in the seventh house of public opinion trine Mercury and Venus. Time and again the critics wrote him off as finished, but the public was faithful, although he made greater demands upon their patience than any other dramatist. He wrote about things and people they understood in words they might have spoken themselves. His plays were lifted whole from American life and from the American cultural and historical tradition. They owed nothing to Europe, and for this reason critics often put O'Neill down as clumsy, inelegant, and sordid.

Although he wrote many plays about social derelicts and outcasts (Moon in Pisces, Neptune in the tenth house) they were devoid of the social criticism and political comment that was so fashionable in the 1920s and 1930s. He accepted society as it was and people as they were; he wrote about both with devastating honesty (Pluto in mutual reception with Mercury). O'Neill's characters are not "products of society" or mouthpieces for propaganda. They are tragic beings whose flaws are in themselves, not in society, however flawed that too may have been.

He wrote always about the intimate relations people had with each other and what they did to each other and to themselves to spoil their lives. In "The Iceman Cometh," the drunken derelicts wait for a tomorrow that will never come, because none of them can leave his past to confront tomorrow. No matter where they had been born, or when, or in what society, they would be doing exactly the same thing in the same way. Society did not make a whore of "Anna Christie": her relation with her father did that, and it was a timeless, eternally repeated relationship that recurs in every society. Nina, in "Strange Interlude" collects three men and plays them off against each other so that she can dominate all their lives. Was there ever a society that did not produce such women? In "Mourning Becomes Electra," he takes a story that the ancient Greeks told about a family caught in the tragedy of the Trojan War. He transposes it in time: his family is caught in the tragedy of the American Civil War. Electra had a father complex in Greece, she had one in America, she will always have one, no matter where or when she is born, or the name of the war from which her father returns to a faithless wife.

The great impact of these plays upon American audiences comes from the fact that, although the themes, the characters, and their tragic flaws are all timeless, they are shown to us in shapes that we have all known intimately. The people on the stage speak the words and the excuses we have all heard a thousand times before, although we have to hear them from O'Neill to understand what they really mean. We've all seen and known the drunks, the whores, the dominating fathers, the distraught children, the unrequited lovers, the slick salesmen. We think of them as distinctively American because they talk our language, but in fact we would have known them anywhere. Had we lived in ancient Egypt, we would have known them there, or in Greece, Rome, China, medieval France, Restoration England, or Soviet Russia. If we are born a thousand years from now, into some still unimagined society, we will know them again, for they are always with us. They are the tragic products of the human dilemma, and their fatal flaws are in us.

Eternal recurrence, eternally impressive and eternally tragic, is a Plutonic concept. People whose charts are dominated by Pluto, like O'Neill's, do not believe in death. They have a psychic awareness of life as an eternal chain. O'Neill's plays are a summing up of the karmic statement, not in terms of myth, theology, religion, or philosophy, but in terms of the everyday life around us, whatever that may happen to be. It is no wonder that critics and self-conscious intellectuals had trouble understanding O'Neill, and that the common people understood him very well.

All of O'Neill's work came out of his own intimate experience, much of it from the traumatic background of his own family. He dug deep in a small mine to bring up treasures no one thought could possibly be there. That again is characteristic of the Pluto dominated chart. His psyche was permanently affected by his relationship with his father and by his mother's tragic addiction to opium (Neptune conjunction Pluto in the tenth house opposition Jupiter in the fourth). The mutual reception of Pluto and Mercury explains why he was able to use his personal suffering constructively, through writing. Where a mutual reception occurs, the astrologer gains insight into how it works by transposing the two planets back into their own signs. Thus Mercury moves into the tenth at 16 Gemini and makes a trine to Uranus in 18 Libra, and Pluto moves back into 5 Scorpio, in the third house of writing and everyday affairs.

That his painful dredging into his own past became the matter of supreme importance to O'Neill is shown by the exact parallel of the Sun and Moon at 9 degrees south, in contraparallel to Pluto at 9 degrees north.

His last three plays, which he never intended should be produced (he left instructions that they be destroyed) were autobiographical. He wrote them, evidently, to resolve the conflicts within himself, to solve the problem of his personal human dilemma, to discover what his own identity (Pluto) really was. They were all produced after his death and they brought him back from the grave to which the critics had assigned him years before when they had pronounced him "finished," a clumsy writer of no real importance who suffered from megalomania because he expected people to sit for five hours looking at plays that didn't seem to say anything we hadn't all heard a thousand times before.

If O'Neill had one consistent theme, it was loneliness: the loneliness of the individual soul that in some mysterious way always made its own fate. To him, this loneliness was tragic because no soul could ever really communicate with another, however great the longing to do so. Each man was himself, and only himself, eternally creating and recreating the fabric of his lives, eternally cutting out the clothes he would wear now and in the future, never able to discard quite all of those he had worn in the past. Again and again O'Neill said that no one can rescue us from ourselves. We are each alone; individuals encased in our Scorpionic shells. Each one of us creates our own life and we go our own way, burdened with the responsibility for what we have made.

No one and nothing outside ourselves will ever rescue us from being what we are. Tomorrow can never come, because today is always the tomorrow we created yesterday.

That is the meaning and message of Pluto. When sex made individuals of us, God removed us from Eden. He was an honest God, however; he had the decency to warn us that the lot we'd chosen for ourselves was not an easy one.

Appendix A

Formula for Casting Johndro Birth Location Charts

The precessional factor for the Right Ascension of the Greenwich Meridian in 1930 was 29° 10'. All calculations begin with this factor. The annual rate of precession is 46"10'. If the birth occurred before 1930, multiply the number of years from birth to 1930 by 46"10' and subtract the result from 29° 10'. If the birth occurred after 1930, perform the same operation, but add the result to 29°10'. This will give you the RAMC for Greenwich in the year desired.

Now take the longitude of the birth place from an atlas or table of geographical longitudes. If the birth occurred east of Greenwich, add this factor to the above sum. If the birth occurred west of Greenwich, subtract it. If the longitude to be subtracted is greater than the RAMC at Greenwich, as it will be for any place in the United States, add 360° before performing the subtraction. This will give you the RAMC for the place of birth in the year desired.

Now take the position of the Sun for the date of birth from the ephemeris for the correct year. Enter a table of right ascensions to discover the R.A. of the Sun for that degree. Add this factor to your previous sum. This will give you the RAMC for the place and date of birth. If more than 360°, subtract the circle.

Enter a table of houses at the point where this degree occurs on the Midheaven for the latitude of the birth place. The cusps corresponding to this degree are the correct Johndro cusps for your birth locality chart.

If you know the hour of birth, figure the correct positions of the planets for that hour and enter them in the chart as you would for any horoscope. If you do not know the hour, enter the planets as shown in the ephemeris for noon or midnight Greenwich, as the case may be. Note on your chart the hour this would be in the place of birth. For instance, if you are using a noon ephemeris, the hour in New York City for the given planetary positions would be 7 a.m.; with a midnight ephemeris, it would be 7 p.m.

29°10′	R.A. Greenwich 1930
− 1 58	Correction to 1776 (154 yrs. X 46".10)
+ 27 52	R.A. Greenwich 1776
+ 360 00	
387 52	
−75 01	Long. Philadelphia
−312 41	R.A. Philadelphia 1776
+ 104 02	R.A. 12 Cancer 56 (Long. Sun at birth)
416 43	
− 360 00	
56 43	R.A. of Birth Locality = M.C. 26 Taurus 43

Entering the tables of houses for latitude 40° North, we find that an M.C. of 26 Taurus 43 yields the following cusps: Ascendant, 2 Virgo 56; second, 26 Virgo 29; third, 25 Libra 05; eleventh, 2 Cancer 51; twelfth, 4 Leo 58.

Appendix B

Source Data for Horoscopes

Foundation Chart of the European Civilization: This horoscope was constructed by Ralph Kraum for December 25, 800 Old Style, at noon, in Rome, Italy. The event was the coronation of Charlemagne.

Adolph Hitler: Born April 20, 1889, at 6:30 p.m. CET, Braunau, Austria.

Donatien Alphonse Francoise, Marquis de Sade: Born June 2, 1740, Paris, France. As the hour of birth is unknown, this is a Johndro birth location chart.

Sigmund Freud: Born May 6, 1856, Freiburg, Moravia (Poland). This chart is #359 in *Sabian Symbols* by Marc Edmund Jones.

United States of America: Horoscope from *Astrological Americana,* Research Bulletin #3 of the American Federation of Astrologers, July 4, 1776, 2:17 a.m. LMT, Philadelphia. The event was the Declaration of Independence.

Gertrude Stein: Born February 8, 1874, Allegheny, Pennsylvania. This is a Johndro birth location chart.

W. Somerset Maugham: Born January 25, 1874, Paris, France. This is a Johndro birth location chart.

Jean Jacques Rousseau: Born April 6, 1670, Geneva, Switzerland. This is a Johndro birth location chart.

Clyde Barrow: Born March 24, 1909, Telico, Texas. This is a solar chart.

Bonnie Parker: Born October 1, 1910, Rowena, Texas. This is a solar chart. Bonnie and Clyde were shot to death in Arcadia, Louisiana, on May 28, 1934.

Albert Henry DeSalvo: Born September 3, 1931, Chelsea, Mass. This is a Johndro birth location chart.

Louis Pasteur: Born December 22, 1822, Dole, France, 2:04 a.m.

Vincent Van Gogh: Born March 30, 1853, 11:00 a.m., Zundert, Netherlands.

Eugene O'Neill: Born October 16, 1888, New York City. This is #740 from *Sabian Symbols* by Marc Edmund Jones.

Karl Marx: Born May 5, 1818, 1:30 a.m., Treves, Germany. #654 in *Sabian Symbols*.

www.ingramcontent.com/pod-product-compliance
Lightning Source LLC
Chambersburg PA
CBHW080516110426
42742CB00017B/3138